Praise for *Unstoppable Teams*

"*Unstoppable Teams* is a valuable reminder of the power of teams. Alden Mills reminds us that if we take care of our team members, we can deliver strong and powerful results, take appropriate risks, and have each other's backs all along the way."
—Arne Sorenson, CEO of Marriott

"Once you've built your team of teams, how can you optimize their strengths? Alden Mills answers this question with specificity, compassion, and dedication. *Unstoppable Teams* is a must-read for any leader hoping to harness the power of relationships in a complex world."
—General Stanley McChrystal (ret.),
founder of McChrystal Group

"*Unstoppable Teams* proves that, with the right leadership, ordinary people can do the extraordinary. Drawing from against-the-odds successes in business ventures and military missions, Mills shares the secrets for building a team that can do the seemingly impossible. Read it and take your team from stuck to unstoppable."
—Liz Wiseman, *New York Times* bestselling author
of *Multipliers* and *Rookie Smarts*

"Alden Mills's over twenty-five years of leadership experience in the military and in business shine through in his practical and memorable book, *Unstoppable Teams*. If you need a guide for building winning teams the right way, you'll find actionable wisdom here."
—Douglas R. Conant, founder and CEO of Conant
Leadership, former CEO of Campbell Soup Company, and
New York Times bestselling author of *TouchPoints*

"The messy business of leadership requires team building. Learn from the best: CEO and Navy SEAL Alden Mills. His CARE framework is refreshing. But you'll never forget the powerful, sometimes painful lessons he shares—from battling asthma to hell week, raising a $30 million bond for schools, and managing the roller coaster of what would become America's fastest-growing consumer-products company. My favorite story is Alden's account, in the last chapter, of his "most terrifying moment." Again and again, Alden reminds us that we all have greater potential than we know if we start engaging the people around us in new, more productive ways. Get a copy of *Unstoppable Teams* and get started."

—Bernie Swain, chairman and founder of the
Washington Speakers Bureau and author
of *What Made Me Who I Am*

"Without a doubt, the most important job of a leader in today's business world is to build exceptional teams. *Unstoppable Teams* is *the* perfect manual for doing just that! Each chapter provides insights, engaging stories, and examples for leaders and those who desire to lead. Alden shows that the best leaders build strong relationships and serve their teams. This refreshing view of leadership is exactly what we need today."

—Mark Lipscomb, vice president of people at 23andMe

"Written with passion, experience, and insight, Alden Mills's *Unstoppable Teams* is for those who want their teams to break away from the rest and lead in their company or industry. If you are looking to develop a team that truly leads the rest, then this book is for you!"

—Sarah McArthur, coauthor of *Work Is Love Made Visible*

"*Unstoppable Teams* stands alone as the most useful handbook for leading teams in complex times—good for a lifetime of inspiration, direction, and purpose. Alden Mills is not just an American hero, he is a motivational genius—blending the excitement and persistence of SEAL training with the wisdom of a road-tested leader. Every company under pressure should have its leaders read this book."

—Brigadier General Tom Kolditz, PhD, founding director of the Doerr Institute for New Leaders, Rice University; professor emeritus at the U.S. Military Academy, West Point; founding director of the West Point Leadership Center; and author of *In Extremis Leadership: Leading as if Your Life Depended on It*

"At first, ordinary teams seem very similar to high-performing teams. Yet there's a critical difference: High-performing teams realize that each team member is different and contributes a specific speciality. Alden Mills discovered a powerful approach to lead you, and your team, to the ultimate performance."

—Sally Hogshead, *New York Times* bestselling author of *How the World Sees You* and *Fascinate*

"*Unstoppable Teams* reminded me how very powerful the emotions of trust; passion; and integrity for people, position, and purpose are with regard to solidifying the infectious nature of a great team. This book is truly an inspiring reminder of how powerful and mighty a team can be, regardless of size. A must-read for leaders at any level."

—Heidi Wissmiller, chief revenue officer of Rodan + Fields

UNSTOPPABLE
TEAMS

THE FOUR ESSENTIAL ACTIONS OF
HIGH-PERFORMANCE LEADERSHIP

ALDEN MILLS

HARPER
BUSINESS

An Imprint of HarperCollinsPublishers

HarperCollins books may be purchased for educational, business, or sales promotional use. For information, please email the Special Markets Department at SPsales@harpercollins.com.

FIRST EDITION

Designed by Nancy Singer

Library of Congress Cataloging-in-Publication Data has been applied for.

ISBN 978-0-06-287615-7

19 20 21 22 23   LSC   10 9 8 7 6 5 4 3 2 1

For my future team leaders:
H-Master, Chow-Chow, Bear, and Yummy

CONTENTS

INTRODUCTION vii

CHAPTER 1 YOUR PLATFORM 1

CHAPTER 2 FINDING UNSTOPPABLES 35

CHAPTER 3 CONNECT 65

CHAPTER 4 ACHIEVE 97

CHAPTER 5 RESPECT 117

CHAPTER 6 EMPOWER 153

CHAPTER 7 ACTIVATING THE 10X ADVANTAGE 177

CONCLUSION 203

ACKNOWLEDGMENTS 211

NOTES 217

INTRODUCTION

"Thah's nah room fah *Rambos* in SEAL Team!"

I can still hear Instructor Smith bellowing that sentence in his thick Bostonian accent, a reference to that ultimate badass, John Rambo, who goes on impossible missions deep behind enemy lines—all by himself—and wins. To our Navy SEAL instructors at BUD/S (Basic Underwater Demolition/ SEAL) school, however, "Rambo" was a pejorative term for the lone wolf who thinks he can do it all himself. Instructor Smith loved repeating that phrase. "Thah's nah room fah *Rambos* in SEAL Team!"

When young men and women who want to join the SEALs first hear about BUD/S, they become obsessed with the grueling physical exertion that lies ahead. But what gets you through the training is a balance of mental, emotional, and physical strength, combined with your greatest asset as a SEAL: the people around you. Instructor Smith's point was clear. It's the team that completes the mission, not some mythical Rambo character.

I know this firsthand: I've led three SEAL platoons, and I've experienced the asymmetrical warfare advantage that SEAL Team cultivates. That advantage has served us in vastly different environments, whether hunting for a war criminal deep in the mountains of Bosnia or conducting classified combat mini-submersible operations at night thirty feet underwater with hand signals (squeezes) as our only means of communication. SEAL Team is bound together by a common purpose and a mentality of "I've got your back." We place the success of the team above individual needs because the team's needs come to represent our individual needs, too.

When a small group of people band together to do something extraordinary, the rest of us scratch our heads in wonder. Whether it's an unranked basketball team outplaying an undefeated powerhouse or a little-known startup becoming the overnight market leader, David and Goliath stories capture our attention and inspire us. We cheer for successful underdogs, and we even dream about being like them—a tightly knit team of ordinary people doing extraordinary things under difficult circumstances. That's what I mean by an unstoppable team, one that brings diverse gifts to bear on the team's goals through a shared sense of purpose and a deep commitment to each other. You can assemble as many individual superstars as you'd like, but they won't become unstoppable unless they believe in each other and in their collective mission.

Unstoppable teams aren't reserved for elite forces in the military. In sports, in business, in communities, in every facet of life, developing the qualities of an unstoppable team is essential if you want to thrive in chaos and break away from the pack. It might sound crazy, maybe even superhuman, but it's within your reach. You don't have to go through BUD/S to build an unstoppable team, but you would do well to incorporate the lessons of team building that have served the legendary Navy SEALs so well for the last fifty-five-plus years. The actions used by SEALs to build high-performing teams are the same actions required in business, nonprofits, and sport teams.

Unstoppable teams come in all shapes and sizes, but they all depend on understanding human emotions, motivations, and values. It is both complex and as simple as this: you must *care*. Caring is the cornerstone for building trust and persistence in any group. When people feel cared for and when they care about the tasks and goals at hand, they are willing to step beyond their perceived limits and dare to do something greater than they originally thought possible.

I've spent the last thirty years daring, failing, and eventually succeeding at building just these sorts of teams—as a member of championship high school and college rowing crews, as a Navy SEAL, as the founder of a successful startup, as a community organizer, and, yes, even as a father and a husband. Though each one of these efforts has had different objectives, they all used the same framework, the same actions, and the same level of "all-in" commitment. If you're willing to commit to caring for and serving others, then you can become a truly unstoppable force for making greatness happen.

Like several other species, humans are preprogrammed to reciprocate when care is bestowed upon us. Open doors for people, and they will respond by opening other doors for other people. This simple act of reciprocity is part of the essential chain reaction that unstoppable teams depend on. Caring unites the head with the heart. However, I'm not talking about simple acts of kindness (though those are essential too); I'm talking about giving your full, authentic commitment to putting others above yourself. That's easier to do when the horizon is clear of danger, but when times get tough, our instinct is to protect ourselves—to seek the cave of safety when the proverbial *T. rex* is chasing us. But if you're able to show care for others only from the safety of your comfy sofa (so to speak), there's no way you can possibly lead an unstoppable team. Unstoppable teams thrive in uncertainty, and let's face it, change and uncertainty are far more common than we'd all like.

So how do you get people to step outside the safety of

their self-interests to join an unstoppable team? From experience and from training, I've identified four actions—connect, achieve, respect, and empower—that, taken together, lie at the heart of every great team. I call it the CARE loop. When these four acts of caring are activated, anything is possible. It's no coincidence that military strategists consider SEALs (and other military special forces) to be force multipliers ten times more effective than conventional troops. Moreover, this extreme team dynamic—what I call the 10x advantage—is not unique to SEAL Teams. It can be harnessed by any well-constructed and highly functioning small team. I have experienced it as a startup founder of one of the fastest-growing consumer-products companies in the country. Much like a SEAL Team, my company's power derived from a handful of people, each with a diverse background and skill set, who went all in on a shared objective: make our core product (the Perfect Pushup device) a category-defining one. The results were staggering: our team created a business that generated nearly $100 million in revenue in just two years and competed against businesses ten times its size.

I also experienced the 10x advantage in sports, as I participated on championship rowing teams in both high school and college. In competitive rowing, arguably the most team-focused sport there is, the difference between winning and losing depends completely on the team performance of eight rowers pulling perfectly in sync. When I rowed for the

US Naval Academy, our crews were predominantly first-time rowers, while the boats of our Division 1 competitors were full of experienced oarsmen (and oarswomen). Yet we routinely competed for championships. We owed this to our ability to build better teams.

Imagine for a moment that you are surrounded by people who will not let you fail. When you see an obstacle, they see an opportunity. When you're scared, they turn to support you. When you're tired, they work tirelessly. When you're uncertain, they reassure you. In short, they make you feel unstoppable. I know this feeling, because I've experienced it time and time again, from the battlefield to the boardroom. You're unstoppable because you share energy that fortifies and focuses each of you, multiplies your strengths, and diminishes your weaknesses.

If you want to be a great team builder, then you need to learn to become a great relationship builder first. It starts with you. In the next chapter, I will discuss the foundational component of every great team: you and the "team" inside of you. Before you can begin to inspire and influence others, you must know yourself and figure out what matters to you. Your "first team" is the only team you can control. In SEAL Team, they call that team your "weapons platform"; I call it your "action platform." Do you think you'll be able to influence, inspire, and convince others to join your quest to accomplish something if you don't come across inspired and convincing? You must first learn to master your own thinking, feelings, and behavior.

Once you learn the drivers of your action platform, chapter 2 will introduce you to the seven traits of unstoppable teammates. Teams are based on relationships, and to build an unstoppable team, you must learn to build relationships with all kinds of people. This is a critical step in your team-building process, because you *want* all kinds of people on your team. The most powerful teams are based on diversity of thought but not of heart. Learning the seven traits of unstoppable teammates will dramatically help you understand how to connect with a wide range of people who can bring a wide range of skills to your team.

In the next four chapters, we will dive into the four-part CARE framework, which lies at the heart of every unstoppable team's success. We'll look at how emotional connections are formed, how goals are established and achieved, why mutual respect can become a renewable resource, and finally how empowerment keeps the team's momentum rolling. With the CARE loop now in your toolbox, we'll turn attention to another group of potential teammates you may be overlooking and undervaluing. These are your customers, your contributors, and your community—the three Cs. By broadening the definition of a team, you'll multiply your team's impact and achieve a 10x advantage against your competitors.

Here's the good news: you don't have to go through a week of sleep deprivation and around-the-clock physical, mental, and emotional harassment to learn these techniques. In BUD/S training, candidates are paired, each person responsible for helping the other get through the training. That's your swim buddy. And that's what I'm going to be for you: your swim buddy. I will be with you each step of the way, encouraging you and challenging you to push past old beliefs in favor of new behaviors that will enable you and your team to do more than you originally thought possible.

Now more than ever, strong teams are needed to solve the challenges of the world. The strength of a company, a community, and even a country depends on great teamwork. The actions detailed in this book are the same ones practiced by Navy SEALs and successful entrepreneurs; they are used by nonprofit leaders, CEOs, coaches, and sports captains. These actions tap into the power of our human spirit and inspire us to go well beyond our perceived limits.

To quote Instructor Smith once more, "Now go hit that surf and get wet and sandy—yah got ninety seconds to make it happen!" The good news is, you don't have to be wet and sandy to turn the page, but you do need to be prepared to dive in headfirst. I am honored to be your swim buddy. I'll see you in the "surf zone" of chapter 1.

Hooyah! (That's SEAL-speak for *Fired Up!*)

UNSTOPPABLE
TEAMS

CHAPTER 1
YOUR PLATFORM

If you didn't pay close attention to his gait, you wouldn't notice his slight limp, and you'd never know he was missing his left butt cheek. Though we never said it out loud, it was hard not to think of him as Instructor Half Ass. In fact, he beat us to the punch, laughingly—and in classic SEAL humor—referring to himself as Instructor Half Ass while reminding us that he could do more with half a butt than we could do with a whole one. I'll never forget the first time I met him. We were about to take our final physical readiness test (PRT), and here was this Vietnam veteran who had left a portion of his body in the muddy waters of the Mekong Delta after miraculously surviving a rocket-propelled grenade ambush. He stood in front of a life-size version of a fictional Hollywood monster, a wooden plaque hanging around its neck with the inscription SO YOU WANT TO BE A FROGMAN.

One hundred twenty-two young men stood at attention in a semicircle around this hero and his sidekick frozen in attack mode. Instructor Half Ass said, "Candidates of Class 181, gather around here. I want to let you in on a little secret."

We shuffled closer to him as he said the word *secret*.

"I want to let you know how to make it through Navy SEAL training. It ain't that complicated, you know." He paused for effect . . . we leaned even closer to hear his answer. "You just have to decide how much you're willing to pay. You see, I happen to know for a fact that about *eighty percent of you aren't going to be willing to pay the price to be a Navy SEAL.*"

He paused again.

"You see, you all want to be a SEAL on a sunny day, *but* your country don't need SEALs on sunny days. She needs them on *scary* days."

As he spoke, I kept thinking the "creature" was going to come alive and support his monologue. He paused a third time.

"When it's cold, dark, and wet and that crack over your head ain't thunder, it's from someone who wants you dead . . . How bad you want to be a SEAL on *that* day?"

He let that question hang for a moment as his eyes scanned the young men standing before him.

"Well, that's my job—to figure out how many of you are willing to pay the price. And you know how I'm going to do it? I'm going to create a conversation between here [pointing to his head] and here [pointing to his heart].

"And I'm going to make this conversation occur the same way those Japanese make a samurai sword." He holds his hands at about stomach level to demonstrate the process.

"You know how they make that sword?"

No one responds, as he cups his left hand.

"They take a hunk of metal, heat it up, and then"—his right hand balls into a fist and slams into his cupped left hand—"then the swordmaker pounds on it. Then he dunks it in cold water. You know how many times he repeats that process to turn that hunk of metal into a sword?"

We slowly swayed our heads back and forth, dreading the answer.

"About two thousand times. I figure that's about how many times we're goin' to do that to you over the next nine weeks in my phase."

He proceeded to tell us how he's going to heat us up, pound on us, and stick us in cold water. He even introduced us to his "hammers," the twenty-five instructors who would be leading us through the first phase of BUD/S.

"Now do yourself a favor and think real hard about how bad you want to be a Navy SEAL before taking this PRT. 'Cause if you pass it, you're moving over to my side of the compound come Monday morning."

Most of us had been anticipating this moment for at

least two years. If you arrived via the Naval Academy, as I had, or a ROTC program, it had taken four years. Those coming from basic training or transferring from a job in the Navy took somewhere between a year and two. We'd already completed two PRTs, and now we were facing our third and final challenge before officially entering SEAL training school. For the past seven weeks, we'd been learning the ropes of being a SEAL candidate, everything from how to wear our vintage World War II uniforms to learning how to perform a "sugar cookie" exercise (hit the surf, then roll around on the beach until covered head to toe in sand). The only thing standing between us and the official start of SEAL training was this one last physical test, the exact same one we'd taken and passed at least twice before. We've got this, right?

After all, we're physically stronger than ever. What's more, we've undergone mental preparations for this moment, encouraged by Instructor Half Ass to tune in to the conversation between our heads and our hearts. As I stood among my fellow candidates, all of them fit and fast, I figured that, athletically, I landed somewhere in the middle of this group of 122 SEAL pledges. Like everyone else, I'd done the PRT twice before, and I wasn't expecting it to be a big deal. But when the test was over, our lead instructor read out the names of those who would be starting SEAL training on Monday morning. I couldn't believe my ears: only 64 of the

122 recruits who had started the program had passed this final PRT test.

How could this be? Why had half the class effectively "decided" not to pass the test? In Instructor Half Ass's words, they had had a conversation with themselves and had made the decision not to pass. They had decided the price to be paid for becoming a Navy SEAL was too great. They'd done the training. They had the skills, but still they'd failed. Their heads (and their bodies) were in it, but their hearts weren't.

I'm sharing this story with you because it highlights the first critical component in building unstoppable teams. The first team you must build and lead is your *own* team, the one inside you. Good ol' Instructor Half Ass hit the nail on the head when he talked about creating a conversation between the head and the heart. That's exactly what's needed to lead oneself.

Though I didn't fully appreciate the wily Vietnam vet's advice at that moment, just a few short weeks later, I found myself engaged in a series of head-to-heart conversations about how much I was willing to give to achieve my goal of becoming a Navy SEAL. Conversations such as the one I had in "drown proofing." That's a game in which your hands are tied behind your back, your feet are tied together, and you're challenged to swim three hundred yards. Two candidates quit before we even got in the pool. Think about this head-heart conversation for a moment. You are instructed to swim without the benefit of the very things that make it possible for you to swim in the first place—your arms and your legs. It's only natural to think, *Hey, wait a second. I need my arms to swim. If I don't have them, then I can't swim.* That's the start of the conversation. Then the head takes the discussion deeper with *Wait, the instructor said you could die doing this. Is this worth it to you?* And then there's the obvious, nagging question: What's the purpose of this test, anyhow? If you allow yourself to fixate on these thoughts, you will create a downward spiral of negative thoughts that can easily lead you to feeling defeated even before you try. Those negative feelings might also cause you to act in a manner that is directly opposed to your goals: you might quit before you even get started.

I learned about the risks of the negative downward spiral the hard way. I was the class leader (and the only officer) of my hell-week class. Class 181 started hell week with thirty-four candidates, thirty-three enlisted and one officer (me). In six days we were down to eighteen candidates, and we still had twenty weeks of basic training to go. It was not a proud moment for me. Here I was in my first true leadership position after four years of leadership training at the Naval Academy, and "my" class had dwindled from sixty-four to eighteen in just the first six of twenty-five weeks of training. All my SEAL instructors made sure I wouldn't forget what poor leadership skills I was demonstrating. They used the group's failing to shine a light on my weaknesses and to force me into yet another conversation with myself about just what a lousy leader I was.

Those conversations were hard. My instructors would present me with a series of facts about how many classmates had quit under my "command." They would ask me repeatedly, "Sir, how can you possibly think you can lead a SEAL platoon when you can't even lead your training class?" Another question they loved to pose: "Sir, we're curious, what does it feel like to be the leader of a class with the most quitters?" They were relentless with their jabs. It bothered me greatly, and they could tell, which made them do it even more. In fact, the closest I ever came to quitting SEAL training had nothing to do with the physical pain; it had to do with the mental anguish of questioning my own ability to lead others. When leading my class through hell week, I often felt self-pity for being the only officer left in the class. My "pity party" featured voices that whined, *This isn't fair— you shouldn't be the only officer* or *Maybe the instructors are right—maybe I'm the liability. Am I the reason everyone's quitting?* These internal voices of self-doubt were fueled by the external voices of my criticizing instructors. I probably would have succumbed to them had I not had a more powerful internal voice motivating me to press on.

Does any of this sound familiar? Have you ever been caught up in self-doubts and self-recriminations at the very moment your team needs you most? Times when you're way out of your comfort zone? You don't need to go through hell week of SEAL training to have this collision of voices directing you to take action away from your desired goal. It's all too easy to obsess about what might go wrong, what you lack, and what bad outcomes could be waiting around the corner. It's all too easy to listen to the negative voices, both those coming from inside your head and from your loudest critics. That kind of noise stops us and, inevitably, our team dead in our tracks. How can you accomplish the task at hand when you're preoccupied with your own thoughts and worries? How can you lead others if you can't even manage yourself?

Your situation may not be as dramatic as the challenges found in SEAL training, but having to handle extreme situations filled with risk and uncertainty is par for the course in every realm these days. How you handle this conversation with yourself—well or not so well—gets amplified when you lead a team. I witnessed it firsthand as I led my SEAL class through hell week. When I was cold and focused on my own misery, my classmates saw it, and they did the same. But when I could redirect my focus to the bigger picture (like leading my team positively through an exercise where failure was a real possibility), my team members were also more likely to gain some perspective on the immediate situation and respond in kind. The ability to lead yourself—what I call your platform—is the foundation for leading unstoppable teams. It doesn't matter if you're sitting in the cold waters of the Pacific Ocean or in the hot waters of a workout division of your bank (where they'd like to repossess your home and bankrupt your company, so they get their money back quicker). The dynamic remains the same: focus on yourself, what you lack, what *you* desire, and you'll get stuck. But focus on what you need to accomplish and how you can enlist others to reach that goal, and you'll become unstoppable. Whatever you do, your actions will be mirrored and magnified by those you lead, and your actions are a result of the conversation ruminating between your head and heart. Learning to lead this conversation—i.e., yourself—is the first step in leading future teammates.

There is perhaps no greater story of the struggle to prevail over competing voices than Sir Ernest Shackleton's heroic leadership of his crew over a two-year journey. In 1914 Ernest Shackleton embarked with twenty-two crew members on the *Endurance* on a quest to be the first explorer to walk across the continent of Antarctica. The trip had been in the making for two years after Norwegian Roald Amundsen became the first to reach the South Pole in 1911. Backed by royalty and various wealthy individuals, and with the support of Winston Churchill, then serving as the first lord of the Admiralty, Shackleton and his hand-selected crew set sail for the island of South Georgia. Fishermen there warned him of the heavy ice floes and suggested he wait another season before attempting his expedition. Indeed, three members of his advance-supply team had already died from his poor leadership and planning. With World War I under way, however, Shackleton didn't want to wait another year to make his historic trans-Antarctic attempt. He set sail for the Weddell Sea (off the coast of Antarctica), where the *Endurance* became trapped in ice from January 24, 1915, until it sank on November 21, 1915. At this point, Shackleton truly began to lead, and what happened next is one of the most remarkable of all stories of human endurance and triumph.

Sir Ernest wrote often of his struggles to keep his crew alive during their perilous journey. After losing the *Endurance*, they sailed over three hundred miles to Elephant Island, then another seven hundred miles while withstanding a hurricane, all in a twenty-five-foot skiff, and finally back to South Georgia. Nancy Koehn, a historian at Harvard Business School, wrote a case study of the leadership techniques of Shackleton during this incredible survival story. She noted in the *New York Times*:

> After the *Endurance* sank, leaving the men stranded on the ice with three small lifeboats, several tents and supplies, Shackleton realized that he himself had to embody the new survival mission not only in what he said and did, but also in his physical bearing and the energy he exuded.[1]

Shackleton suffered his own doubts from time to time but never let on to his crew. He was the first to make sacrifices on behalf of the crew. He made a point of leaving his gold pocket watch on the ice when he commanded everyone else to leave all nonessential items behind. He gave his mittens to his photographer, Frank Hurley, eventually suffering frostbitten fingertips. He helped make the meals and ensured that everyone ate every four hours. He often took back-to-back watches so his men could rest longer, and he always broke trail for them. As one of his crew, Frank Worsley, described his boss's attitude, "It was his rule that any deprivation should be felt by himself before anybody else."

When Shackleton finally returned to England with his entire crew, his expedition had been considered a failure, yet his crew considered him a savior. They would not have survived were it not for his focus on first leading himself. He knew that his personal actions would be the deciding factor in keeping his crew alive.

Very few of us will ever have to face the hardships that the captain and crew of the *Endurance* encountered. That's not the point of reminding you of Shackleton's story; it's to impress upon you the importance of a leader's focus, because it determines the team's outcome. Had Shackleton and his crew greeted the ice floes with dismay and negativity—an easy mind-set to embrace, considering that their ship was lost along with their expedition's trans-Antarctic goal—the outcome most assuredly would have been death. Shackleton's ability to focus his internal conversation on seeking success versus feeling sorry for himself and the predicament he'd put his team in directly affected the morale and focus of his crew. We have all encountered moments when our mind-sets and emotions are conflicted, when our head tells us to stop and our heart tells us to keep going. It's these very "conversations" that I'm encouraging you to have with yourself. They will bring you clarity about your purpose and your direction and enable you to bring that clarity to your actions and to your team.

I have never experienced the challenges of navigating a twenty-five-foot skiff over nearly a thousand nautical miles in the frigid waters off Antarctica, but I did experience my own "Shackleton moment" in business, and it lasted nearly as long as it took the *Endurance* captain to get his crew home safely. Here's the story: Shortly after my company, Perfect Fitness, was recognized by *Inc.* magazine as the fastest-growing consumer-products company in the United States (number four overall), our bank froze our credit line. Now, I'm not trying to play the victim here. We had just told bank managers that we were going to break a couple of covenants in our credit contract, and it was March 2009, the height of the global economic downturn. We had a $15 million line of credit; we owed $8.8 million and had been with this bank for only six months when it decided we weren't a fit any longer.

The bankers wanted us to pay them back within thirty days. Their focus, which was the focus they wanted us to have, was "how much of their money can the bank get back in the next thirty days?"

They were willing to negotiate with us as to how much we would pay them back. Had we accepted their focus, we would have been bankrupt on the thirty-first day, the day after we paid them back. *Our* focus, however, was on weathering what became a perfect storm of events, from our bank's twitchiness to the shifting retail landscape to the volatility of the financial markets. In the bank's defense, its concerns were not without merit. In the previous three months, our sales had dropped radically, due to changes in the marketplace. So, focusing on what the bank was going to lose made sense—for the bank. But for my team, the focus had to be on survival, on how to adapt to the changes and come out stronger and ready to make new moves. There were plenty of other lessons I would learn from this crisis, but for now the one I want to impress upon you is this: where you put your focus will determine your actions. We chose to put our focus on convincing the bank that we needed more time, not on trying to get discounts on our loan balance. We created a specialized team to get the bankers to align their focus with ours. And guess what happened. Day by day, week by week, the banking team slowly shifted its focus to *our* focus of paying the bank back in full over a longer period. Eleven months later, we repaid every dime while keeping the company alive and growing our product line.

As an entrepreneur, I could ride this wave of uncertainty because I'd been there before. As with my SEAL instructors, the bankers kept telling us that we wouldn't make it. Quit now, they said, because that's your only option. Nevertheless, *our* focus drove us to take different actions—to find ways to keep our company afloat and growing. We had built our own unstoppable team while dealing with an obstacle that a lot of so-called experts said was insurmountable. Each time you confront a challenge, whether it's sitting in cold water or getting out of hot water, the first thing you must do is take charge of the conversation inside your head. You need to build a strong platform to lead others. You need to be able to keep your focus steady even when the voices around you are telling you to quit. And you need to be able to inspire your team members to shut those voices out too.

In the age of social media and the twenty-four-hour news cycle, learning how to tune in to what really matters has never been more important. For insight and inspiration, I often turn to the now classic example of James E. Burke, the CEO of Johnson & Johnson from 1976 to 1989. Six years into his tenure, Burke faced a challenge that could have bankrupted J&J, a company founded in 1887. In 1982 seven people in the Chicago area died from cyanide-laced Tylenol capsules that an anonymous culprit had put on retail shelves. At the time, Tylenol had a whopping 35 percent share of a $1.2 billion analgesic market. Lives were at risk, and so was the company's future.

Burke assembled a seven-person team to focus on handling the threat, but it was his leadership directive that changed the course of the crisis and eventually led the way for innovation and opportunity. The forty-year J&J veteran recounts his decision as a "conversation" that his team was struggling with: saving lives *and* saving Tylenol. Burke recalls, "Whenever we cared for the customer in a profound and spiritual way profits were never a problem."[2]

He made a series of profound decisions. He ordered a recall of every single bottle of Tylenol—over thirty-one million bottles in total. He made daily calls to the chiefs of all major news stations to keep them informed of what his company was doing. He tasked his teams to create new tamper-proof bottles and stopped distribution of Tylenol until the new caps were ready. Tylenol market share plunged to 7 percent in the weeks following his decision, but as word spread about J&J's response to the crisis, sales rebounded. By the end of 1982, Tylenol's market share had climbed back to 30 percent, and by the following year, it reached 35 percent. Mr. Burke's decision would eventually bring him to the White House to be honored with the highest civilian award, the Presidential Medal of Freedom. When asked about how he grappled with that decision, he referenced the company's now famous credo, which explicitly places the needs of customers above those of shareholders: "The credo made it very clear at that point exactly what we were all about. It gave me the ammunition I needed to persuade shareholders and others to spend the $100 million on the recall. The credo helped sell it."[3]

The conversation that leaders need to have with themselves, between their hearts and their heads, is ongoing—and that's a good thing. It's healthy and productive for leaders to examine their own thoughts and beliefs—to find a way to reconcile those internal conversations with the needs and goals of the team.

The easiest and often the most logical thing to do is to quit or to compromise, even if doing so works against your long-term goals. But that's not what courageous leaders like Shackleton and Burke did. Instead, they took those voices into account, but then redirected their energies and their team's efforts to the horizon, to the larger principles, values, and aspirations that mattered most. Remember: focus drives your actions, and your actions are emulated by your team. Lead yourself first, and then you'll be able to lead your team.

THE FORMULA: FOCUS, FEEL, ACT

There are only three things you can control: your mental, emotional, and physical capabilities. That's it. We can't control the weather, our competition, the marketplace, or our employees. Heck, as parents we can't even control our kids! But we can control what we think, how we feel, and how we act and/or react to what comes our way. Put simply, focus on what you can control, and decide what you want to react to. Period. What we act on is totally dependent on what we focus on.

The Focus, Feel, Act formula works for individuals, but it's also how unstoppable leaders build 10x teams. What we focus on creates a feeling that drives a behavior that results in an action. The resulting action either reinforces our focus and feeling or shifts them to take a different action. The challenge is trying to make sense of all those internal voices.

Have you ever heard of this saying: "It's darkest before dawn"? (It is a true statement, by the way; it is coldest just before dawn too!) The point is, these voices can become very distracting when you are in the "darkest" of places. If you don't know how to recognize which voices to listen to, you could fall victim to the wrong one and never see the first light of your success. Learning what drives these voices and how to harness them to your advantage will give you and those who join your team a massive advantage in becoming unstoppable.

THE WHINER, THE WHISPERER, AND THE ACTOR

Our brains are over two million years old, but in some respects they haven't changed much over time. Neuroscientific research confirms that, first, our brains are preprogrammed for self-preservation; second, they are lazy; and, third, vital chemicals produced in our body have a dramatic impact on how we think and feel. Much of human history has been a struggle for survival in harsh environments. And despite the far more luxurious circumstances most of us in the developed nations live in today, our brains are still operating as if the world were just as perilous, and thus our brains try to keep us focused on avoiding risks, on self-protection, and on fight-or-flight responsiveness.

When I say our brains are lazy, I mean that they are endlessly focused on conservation—energy conservation, that is. Energy (calories) is precious to our prehistoric brains, in part because food was sometimes scarce. Thinking requires a great deal of energy, so seeking the simplest solution is in our best interest. The brain is remarkably adept at creating reasons *not* to do something. How many times have you thought, *What's the point of this?* or *Why should I do this?* or *Who else has done this?* These responses are the brain's way of trying to conserve energy by avoiding risks and new challenges.

Finally, our brains' functional capabilities are directly dependent on three things: nutrition, sleep, and exercise. These three pillars dramatically influence brain function, and they are all interconnected. You know the old saying "You are what you eat." Now think of a more verbose but more inclusive version: "What you eat, how well you sleep, and how often you move is how you think." Eat potato chips, Twinkies, and pasta all day, and you'll become mentally sluggish and slow to process complicated tasks after the sugar rush wears off. The same goes for sleep. Have you ever stayed up for twenty-four hours straight? How about forty-eight or seventy-two hours? As part of SEAL training, I've stayed up for over ninety-six hours. Do you know what happens when you do this? You hallucinate. Brains need sleep to function. And the better the sleep, the better they function. The same goes for exercise. When our heart rate rises during exercise, circulation improves, which means more blood flow to the brain. Blood carries nutrients and oxygen along with critical hormones that stimulate brain function. (For more on this, see an insightful book called *Spark: The Revolutionary New Science of Exercise and the Brain* by John J. Ratey with Eric Hagerman.)

But what, you may ask, does any of this have to do with team building? Knowing how the brain works helps you understand how to help others stay focused on what matters most. The brain is cunning. It's always trying to convince you and your teammates not to press on, not to venture into the unknown, not to go against the advice of the crowd. Appreciating why our brains function the way they do is extremely helpful in understanding how to "convince" it to work for, not against, our goals. Your brain will always be a bit of a whiner, but you can stem some of its complaining by feeding, resting, and exercising it. You can also keep those whiny complaints in check by learning to manage another critical component of your platform: your emotions.

There are lots of discussions on exactly where our emotions come from, but for the sake of simplicity, I will use "heart" and "gut" interchangeably as the general location of our emotions. The adage "Trust your gut" has now been scientifically proven. Turns out we have a second brain in our gut. The exact same neurons in our brain exist in our gut; the only difference is we have over eighty billion neurons in our head and a little over five hundred million neurons in our abdomen. Our brain has lots more communicating cells, neurons, than our "heart" or "gut" does. The effects of our emotions on our actions may seem subtler—that's why I refer to them as the whisperer—but their impact is perhaps even greater.

Remember a time when you did something wrong, and you knew it was wrong, but you did it anyway? I have many moments I can use as examples, but here is one of my earliest ones, which I can still remember as if it was yesterday. When I was a child, my favorite outdoor activity was hunting for frogs, snakes, and turtles. I would ride my bike down to a pond on a public golf course, wait for golfers to tee off, and then troll the shoreline hoping to sneak up on a bullfrog, snake, or turtle. I loved the sport of catching them and the excitement of bringing one home as my newest pet.

One day, an older kid arrived at the pond and showed me his technique for catching bullfrogs. He used a long stick to whack the back of the unsuspecting bullfrog. The teenager promised me that it didn't hurt the frog; it merely "knocked it out" just long enough for him to grab it. I was thrilled with this new technique and set out to try it on a bullfrog that had eluded me for weeks. In the past, I'd never been able to get closer than a few feet before it jumped to safety into the middle of the pond. But now armed with my long stick, I could sneak up and whack him just as the older boy had instructed. To my delight, it worked! The big old frog didn't move as I scurried into the muck to capture my prize. There was this moment for me of absolute pride followed by a sickening feeling in my stomach that grew with every second this frog didn't wake up. Seconds turned into minutes as the frog remained in his "knocked-out" state.

My joy quickly turned into a sobbingly sad moment. I had killed the very frog I had hoped to bring home and take to school for show-and-tell. I was sick to my stomach, crying like a baby, and I swore to myself that I would never use this stick-whacking technique again. That was over forty years ago. I don't remember the name of the boy who showed me how to use the stick, and I don't remember the date or the day of the week, but I remember everything about how I felt when I killed that frog. I remember carrying the dead frog home. I remember showing my mom the body. I remember her helping me bury it. I cried myself to sleep that night.

I offer this story as a simple example of the power of emotion. Emotions may speak softly, but they can be demanding, often overriding the logic our brains are presenting. Have you ever heard of or witnessed someone doing a heroic feat in the face of extreme danger, such as running into a burning building to save someone? Or how about the soldier who runs back into the line of fire to rescue a wounded platoon mate? Examples of emotion-driven outcomes are all around us, especially when it comes to sports (not to mention romance, gambling, and disco dancing). And emotions play a bigger role in the workplace than anyone cares to admit. We like to pretend that rationality, logic, and reason rule the day in business, but the reality is that most decisions and actions depend just as much on emotions—the way leaders self-regulate theirs (or not!) and the way they deploy them to inspire their teams.

The myriad feelings that flow through our minds minute by minute add up to our emotions: love, hate, anger, sadness, regret, happiness, caring . . . These feelings can jump into the driver's seat and steer us into taking the ugliest courses of action, such as hurting others or ourselves; conversely, these feelings can drive us to take actions that save lives and bring joy to people. Out-of-control emotions are like driving a car without ever taking your foot off the gas. You're eventually going to crash or hurt someone else. But if you learn to regulate your emotions, to direct your attention to productive emotions, you will learn to drive like a Formula One champion, expertly banking the curves, learning when to hold back and when to let go as new crises and opportunities appear.

Now that we've covered the first two components of the Focus, Feel, Act formula, let's turn to the third. You may be surprised to learn that when you join the military, you are not immediately shown how to hold a gun or make your bed or even how to salute. The very first lesson you learn is how to stand. Instructors break down the proper military stance into several small actions, starting with your feet. They want your heels together while your toes point out at 35 degrees, knees slightly bent, chest out, shoulders rolled back, arms at your side, fingers rolled inward with no fingernails showing, chin up, and eyes forward. Posture is a big deal in the military, and it's not just for looking sharp on the parade ground. Your physical posture doesn't just communicate your military bearing to others; it also activates how you feel.

Sound crazy?

Try this drill: look down to the ground, put your chin on your chest, roll your shoulders forward while hunching your back. Do you feel powerful? How about confident? Now take a couple of steps while in this downward-facing posture. Do your steps have energy or are you shuffling your feet? Now try having a conversation in this position. How do you come across? What does your voice sound like? Do you think you sound convincing? Think you could sell something standing and feeling like this? Of course not. You look beaten down, you lack energy, and you're moping and mumbling like someone having a pity party.

Now switch your posture to match the military instructions I just outlined. A series of physiological reactions begin to take effect, from blood flow to airflow. Your body's position directly affects your state of being. You now can use the full range of your vocal cords and windpipe because your chin is up, which allows optimal airflow into your lungs. Your back is straight, your hips are aligned, and your knees are bent, enabling optimal blood circulation throughout your body. Within seconds a new feeling takes shape: you feel confident, proud, and strong. Now take a step. How do you walk? Can you feel the power transfer from each foot as it pushes off the ground and propels you forward? Now strike up a conversation with someone, or even with yourself while looking in a mirror. What does your voice sound like? Confident, perhaps even commanding. Which posture do you think would help you more in selling something or convincing someone to join you on a dangerous mission or a journey into the unknown (e.g., team building)?

Our ability to talk back to the whiner (the brain) and listen to the whisperer (our emotions) is directly linked to our physical actions. Posture is just the starting point. Try giving a speech sitting in a chair, and then try giving the same speech standing up. Which position do you think will make for a more compelling delivery? Speaking of sitting down, try having a conversation sitting upright and leaning forward. Now slouch in your chair lounging backward. How does your energy level change? Think you would be effective at doing math problems in this laid-back position? Here's another simple one. Are you more engaging standing still or moving? Try walking and talking versus sitting and talking. Which one makes you feel more engaged? Hint: it all has to do with increased blood flow to the brain.

As Instructor Smith loved to remind us in his thick Boston accent, "Thah bodee ain't notin' more than ah brain-housin' group." His point was that our entire body supports the functions of our brain. It's responsible for feeding our brain oxygen and the proper nutrients and also for carrying out the brain's commands, i.e., taking action. The condition of our body determines how much work we can accomplish. Work described as a scientific equation is mass multiplied by acceleration multiplied by distance. Our body's ability to handle a sustained workload, also referred to as stamina, affects several mental and emotional drivers, such as what we think we can do and what we feel (believe) we can try. Think about this for a moment. If you walk up a flight of stairs and find yourself gasping for air, how do you think your brain interprets this? Do you think your brain would respond with "Hey, let's go climb a mountain"? No, of course not. Your brain is going to side with your body, focus on how hard you were breathing, and amplify the situation with a response such as "Whoa, next time take the escalator, so we can avoid a potential heart attack."

Here's the catch: If you allow yourself to accept the easy way out, your brain will continue to seek reasons not to do the extra work, and your body will follow suit and get even more out of shape. However, if you focus your brain on how to climb those stairs faster, your brain will seek more efficient ways to move the body up the stairs. Do this routine a few times, and you will start a positive chain reaction. Your heart rate will get elevated enough to produce the feel-good hormones (dopamine and serotonin) that excite the neurons in the brain to build new pathways and positive associations between "feeling good" and "climbing stairs."

The process of building new neural pathways is like creating a new path in a dense jungle.[4] The first time out is tough going; every step is hard because you're hacking your way with a machete through tangled vegetation. However, if you return the next day to the same path, it's easier. Some of the vegetation might have snapped back into place but you're not whacking nearly as many branches out of the way. Do this repeatedly day after day, and your path turns into a well-marked trail. The more you travel this route, the easier and faster it gets. This is the same thing that happens inside your brain when you try something new. The first time is usually the hardest. I say usually, because if we're trying to do something new to us, many times the first time is a failure—the path isn't even complete—and we don't get the satisfaction of completing our path through the "jungle." This is where the body can help us try again. Though we may have failed, the body doesn't know the difference between success and failure; it knows only work. The more work we do, the stronger we get, and the more of those healthy hormones get produced. It's up to our mental and emotional drivers to decide what our body does. If we task our bodies to do too much too soon, our body shuts down (i.e., "bonks"—runs completely out of energy). However, if our body is conditioned for the workload, it can provide the positive feedback to our mental and emotional drivers to keep going.

Whether you are climbing stairs or selling widgets, the same rules apply. Your body plays an influencing role in deciding what to focus on and linking how you feel with your actions. This three-way conversation between our mental, emotional, and physical "voices" is always going on. Understanding these influencers is paramount to leading your first team: you. So how do you get these individual "voices" to team up to work as one?

WHY IT MATTERS

The key to making your mental, emotional, and physical platform work for you is understanding *why* you care. Take the
two stories at the beginning of this chapter, enduring SEAL
training and facing bankruptcy with my first company. In
SEAL training, why did so many stronger and faster candidates quit, while others who weren't as fast or as strong
stick it out? I can't speak for all of them, but I know why I
kept going. My focus was on what I cared about. I wasn't focusing on being a SEAL on a "sunny day"; I focused on all
those people who said I couldn't do it. I thought about the
doctor who diagnosed me with asthma as a child and who
suggested I live a less active lifestyle and learn the game of
chess. I thought about the people I cared about most, such
as my parents and brother, and how they would feel if I quit.
Every time I found myself in the darkest of moments, when
the "conversation" turned into an argument inside of me,
I would focus my thoughts on why I cared about making it
through SEAL training. Every time I found myself close to
the edge of quitting, I focused on the people I cared about
most and the impact my failure would have on them and
me. That focus would generate a feeling so unacceptable
that I always found the strength to keep going. Later, when
my startup was facing bankruptcy, the people I cared about
most were (are) my wife and children. I would walk into my

children's room, watch them sleeping, and think of myself quietly saying, "Boys, Daddy quit today." I would role-play this conversation while staring at them. I could hear them say, "Why, Daddy?" and "What does this mean, Daddy?" I would explain that it means we have to move far away and start over. Each time I role-played that conversation and focused on the negative outcome of the situation I was in at the time, a feeling so awful swelled inside my gut that I would always find the resolve to take another action to overcome the obstacle at hand.

Whether you are training to endure physical pain, grappling with a mental challenge, or struggling with an emotional issue, understanding why you care about overcoming the obstacle is your most powerful weapon. Each time I find myself staring into the abyss of one of these obstacles, my greatest strength comes from my focus and understanding of why I care.

We are wired to care for others. Our care is most powerful when we link it with an individual and personalize it. The power of our care loses its influence as we expand its scope. For example, if you're trying to raise money for charity, what do you think is a more powerful connection, telling a personal story about a child's challenges (better still, having that child tell his story) or telling a general story about a large group of people in need? We connect at the individual level first and foremost. The same thing occurs when dealing with those demons of self-doubt. In SEAL training, I thought of specific family members; in business my focus was on my wife and children. In both cases, I would focus on people I cared about most. Connecting your care at the individual level is the secret to knocking back those demons of doubt and convincing your platform to press on.

For years I would go through this informal process of determining why and what I care about when the struggle grew to the point of questioning why I was doing something. I found myself having these circular conversations. Sometimes they would spiral upward; other times, they would take me into a nose dive. A turning point in my SEAL training came while I was on a three-mile open-water ocean swim about four weeks after completing hell week. I had been sneaking asthma medication during training because I felt that it would help me (by that point I had been taking it for over ten years). On this day, however, something was wrong, really wrong. I know a three-mile swim sounds long, but when you're using fins and have a swim buddy facing you, it's not nearly as daunting as it sounds. Swims were one activity most of us looked forward to because it's a guaranteed hour or more where instructors aren't hassling you. But this swim was different for me.

My lungs were struggling for air. It felt as if I were breathing through a straw partially full of liquid. The fluid blocking my airway was making my breathing sound more like gurgling. About halfway through, my swim buddy looked at me and said, "Hey, Millsy, there's blood on your lips. Are you all right?" The fluid filling up my lungs was blood. I felt I was drowning. Within minutes I was pulled from the water, removed from my class, and brought to medical. Hours later and after several tests, including a comprehensive blood test, they discovered my crutch—the asthma medication. The lead doctor said, "Ensign Mills, asthmatics aren't allowed in SEAL training. You have asthma and you shouldn't be here. It's remarkable you made it as far as you did, but this is the end of the line. You have nothing to be ashamed of. You're not quitting, you're being medically dropped from BUD/S."

I remember thinking just for a second how simple and logical this all sounded. It was an easy path to take; it saved my pride and provided me with the perfect excuse to everyone who mattered most: a medical malady. But I didn't take that path. I refused it. I pushed back and politely told the doctor that I didn't have asthma and was only using the medication to help me recover from a lung infection I got in hell week.

He was furious. He pulled me from my class, put me on what is called a medical hold, and sent me to the main military hospital in San Diego for a full asthma evaluation. This process took more than a week, and I had five more weeks to wait until I would learn my fate: either receiving a medical discharge or being allowed to join the next SEAL class. I had lots of free time to reflect on my situation, and it was during these days that I created a process for dealing with challenges, especially ones that feel outside of my control. I call this process making an outcome account, and I have used it for every single hardship I have faced since that day I was pulled from the water and almost forced out of SEAL training. (I passed the asthma test, called a methacholine challenge, wherein they put you in a sealed box and measure your lung volume before and after spraying an asthma-inducing mist into your lungs. How I passed is another story but, suffice it to say, that was the day I stopped taking all forms of asthma medication.)

Here's how the outcome account works. Draw a capital T on a blank piece of paper and define your goal on top of the T. Be as specific as possible. In the case of SEAL training, I wanted to graduate with the next class: Class 182. Put a plus sign on one side of the vertical line of the T and a minus sign on the other. Then answer three questions:

1. What is the outcome of achieving this goal (i.e., what happens to you)?
2. Who is affected by this outcome?
3. How does it make you feel?

You will answer these questions twice, once assuming you reach the goal and once assuming you don't. The more you can visualize your feelings—and the impact your success or failure will have on other people—the more useful the exercise will be. If you do not feel a physical "pit" growing in your stomach when thinking about not achieving this goal, then either you are not visualizing creatively enough or the goal is not that important to you after all. When I was thinking of quitting SEAL training, I would conjure up thoughts on what it would feel like in twenty years telling my kids why "Daddy quit" and saying, "Don't do what Daddy did." Really push yourself on finding horrible and happy feelings on both sides of the outcome. Here's a sample outcome account for you.

Outcome Accounts:

Define your goal

+	−
1.	1.
Outcomes	Outcomes
2.	2.
Impact	Impact
3.	3.
Feel	Feel

The outcome account provides you with a framework for discovering why you care. As you go through this process, you will discover that putting your attention on bringing joy to those you care about most versus letting them down will become your strongest source of inspiration. The outcome account brings clarity to your platform and helps you lead the conversation with yourself in a more orderly fashion. It helps remove the whining from your head and heighten the whispers of your heart. Knowing what you care about and how it makes you feel will help you focus on taking the actions required to succeed. Becoming an unstoppable leader begins with understanding yourself.

CHAPTER 2

FINDING
UNSTOPPABLES

When I was growing up, one of my favorite Saturday-morning cartoons was *Super Friends*. The show was based on a collection of well-known superheroes, including Superman, Wonder Woman, Aquaman, and Batman and Robin. As the show grew in popularity, more superheroes emerged, such as the Flash, Cyborg, Green Lantern, and my favorite duo, the Wonder Twins. All these characters had different powers and weaknesses. Superman could fly and see through walls but was powerless against kryptonite. Aquaman could breathe underwater and harness the power of the oceans but lost his power out of the water. Batman and Robin had special inventions for all kinds of missions, like the Batmobile and Batcopter, but they were still human. Wonder Woman had superhuman strength and speed and could stop bullets with bulletproof bracelets, but she herself was not impervious to injury. By the time *Super Friends* ended, more than twenty different superheroes had joined forces to battle the most unimaginable villains. These demonic bad guys (and gals) had more superpowers than any one Super Friend, but they lacked one critical power: the ability to team up. Each show had a similar theme: a single superhero tries to take on the villain, gets captured (or is about to meet his or her demise), and then must rely on a team of Super Friends to deploy their various superpowers to destroy the villain.

Super Friends was fun to watch because there was no one superhero who could do it all; each needed the others to save the world. Sometimes they would fight among themselves, but when the fate of the world hung in the balance, they harnessed all their powers in unison to win. *Super Friends* might have been the first cartoon to depict superheroes teaming up, but the theme is as old as the Greeks. Three thousand years ago, the Greeks invented their own "Super Friends" characters to captivate people; they called them gods and goddesses. The cast included eight gods and six goddesses with all kinds of different godlike powers, ranging in pleasantness from Aphrodite, the goddess of beauty and love, to Ares, the god of war. Poseidon, god of the sea, and Zeus, king of the gods, had more power than the rest.

There was also a common villain, Hades, god of the under-world. When the gods and goddesses were challenged, they, too, teamed up to defeat the dark powers of the underworld. No single Greek god or goddess was all-powerful; the powers of each one complemented those of the others. United, they were unstoppable.

Do you see my point? All great teams are made up of people with complementary skills and strengths. You may not think of your analytical proclivity to manipulate spread-sheets as a superpower, but if we worked together, I would be the first to acknowledge it. Spreadsheets give me hives. OK, maybe not, but I do get in a panic just at the thought of dealing with them. The person who loves pivot tables and data analysis might feel like vomiting at the thought of hav-ing to lead a sales presentation. Sure, these "powers" might not be as glamorous as leaping over tall buildings or breath-ing underwater, but they are real skills and talents, critically important to grow a company or save one from bankruptcy. I have led in both growing and saving a company, and the only way we defeated the competition and beat back bankruptcy (the villains) was by creating teams of people with comple-mentary skills.

It might sound as though all you need to do is get a group of people with different skills together, and—presto!—you have an unstoppable team. But building unstoppable teams is challenging. For one thing, our egos, our pride and insecurities, may prevent us from seeing where our true powers (and our real weaknesses) lie. Second, it's not always easy to recognize other people's superpowers. Third, it can be a challenge for individually gifted people to see the benefit of working with others to accomplish a common goal. A lot of high-achieving people get that way through a single-minded focus on themselves and their goals. Convincing them to pursue "our" goal instead of "my" goal is no small feat.

Likewise, a lot of team leaders are not being honest with themselves about their own strengths and weaknesses. Most of us think we are better at more things than we really are. It is hard to come to grips with our own weaknesses. It is no fun discussing what we stink at; on the other hand, we all love thinking and talking about moments when we saved the day, scored the goal, or made the sale. We tend to overemphasize our own participation and marginalize everyone else's involvement—unless and until, that is, you decide to become unstoppable. Truly understanding your gifts will help you not only realize your full potential, but also identify your weaknesses. When you know this, then you can get to work seeking other Super Friends to join you on an unstoppable team.

GETTING REAL WITH YOURSELF

Sometimes our own superpowers aren't obvious to us. That's why relying on others to help you identify your strengths and weaknesses can be helpful. I call this triangulating, after the technique of land navigation that we learned during SEAL training (it's also taught in wilderness survival classes). When you're lost in the woods but have a map and a compass, you can triangulate to discover your position. As long as you can climb a tree or get to some other suitable vantage point, it's simple. Locate three immovable objects around you that are plotted on the map, such as a mountain, a bend in a river, and a huge rock. Now use your compass to shoot a bearing from each object. Draw a line on your map representing each bearing of your compass, and you'll notice that they form a small triangle where they intersect, hence the term *triangulation*. Your location is inside the triangle. See the figure below for an example.

Triangulation

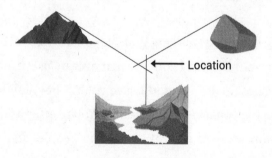

← Location

This method for finding your location in the woods can be adapted to helping you discover your true skill. Here are the steps.

STEP ONE: Find at least three people from three different environments of your life to give you honest feedback. Select people who will give it to you straight without fear of hurting your feelings. When you select these people, find one or two people each from your professional life, your personal life, and your community. Do you volunteer? Go to church? Coach? Participate in a fantasy football league? Have yoga friends? Whatever your interests, find one or two people who best represent your community. On the personal side, I rely on my wife for critical feedback and boy, she doesn't hold back! You might ask a parent or a grandparent, an old coach, a new teacher, or a close friend. In any case, seek out one or two people from your personal life whom you can count on for no-holds-barred feedback. On the work front, find one or two colleagues who don't directly report to you, but with whom you have worked or are working closely.

STEP TWO: Ask them this question: "If you were counting on me to save your life but I could save it only by using the one thing I am best at, how would I save you?" They should answer by giving you a verb, not a noun. You're after the verb. What action are you best at—inspiring people, analyzing data, drawing pictures, coordinating a project, inventing a new idea, or . . . ? Get them focused on the one thing above all else that you are hands down the best at. The goal is to find "your" verb—the action that others view as your great-est strength.

STEP THREE: Triangulate the feedback and look for similar-ities, commonalities, and patterns in it. Test the feedback against your own answers to these questions. Is there some-thing in the feedback that rings true in your gut, not just your head? Does some portion of the feedback sound familiar to you? Have you heard it before? When you were younger, did people say of you, "He's a natural leader," or "What a gift he has for art," or "She's like a human computer doing complex math in her head"?

This exercise helps you identify your own talents and also the skill gaps you'll need to fill with contributions from teammates. You may even find people who are better than you at the one thing you know you're great at. Don't despair; they will only give your team more depth. It's convenient to say to yourself, *I don't need to do this exercise. My team is hum-ming right along.* That's what I thought until my team wasn't humming right along. The best time to do this exercise is when things are going well. Don't let the humming lull you into complacency. Always be evaluating whether you have the right skills and the right people in the right jobs. Iron-ically, I didn't do this drill until I found myself questioning my abilities while my company was floundering. I was asking myself, *Am I as good as I think I am?* Self-doubt prompted me to reach out to others I trusted. When I asked this question of my "community," the feedback was on the order of "You'd fire me *up* to save me" and "You'd motivate me to get unstuck." All the responses I was getting were about inspiring others, and yet my role was supposed to be leading innovation. Something was off. I didn't want to embrace it at first, but as the company continued a downward spiral, I removed myself as "chief innovator" and brought in someone whose superpower was innovating. And I'm glad I did. Within months, our product line expanded and sales grew. My only regret was that I didn't do it earlier!

This exercise gives you a mirror into your true strengths and weaknesses, and because you're getting feedback from others who see you in action, the picture you get is truer to life than the one you might selectively present to yourself. Yes, you have to trust others to tell you what they're seeing. Eventually you'll see their honesty as a gift, because that "reflection" can dramatically improve your chances for success.

THE SEVEN UNSTOPPABLE TRAITS

Most athletes who play collegiate sports have practiced their sport for at least four years before entering college; many began playing long before high school. This is especially true if you play in a Division 1 (D1) college athletic program. D1 National Championships feature the best athletic teams in the country, and many college athletes go on to become Olympians and/or professionals. That's not the case, however, if you go to the US Naval Academy and join the rowing team.

In the hypercompetitive world of D1 college sports, most coaches spend hundreds of hours combing the world for recruits to compete on their teams. Not Navy Crew. Sure, they get a few blue-chip athletes, but Navy athletes are there first and foremost to become naval officers, not to play college sports. The Naval Academy, like the other service academies, is not your normal college experience. For starters, it's a regimented military environment where most academic studies are heavily concentrated on engineering topics. Then there's the six-year commitment to serve in the armed forces upon graduation. It's not for everyone. The young men and women who apply have to really want to go to one of these institutions.

When I was admitted to the Naval Academy, I was one of the few recruits who had rowing experience. I had rowed crew for four years in high school and had won practically every race in our New England division. I thought I was pretty good at rowing. I even showed up a week late for Plebe Summer at the Naval Academy because my high school crew had been invited to compete internationally. (By the way, I don't recommend showing up a week late at any service academy.

I was so behind in training that I spent the entire summer trying to catch up—and never really did!) So imagine my surprise when I arrived at the Navy boathouse to meet my new teammates. Only three of them had ever rowed before.

Most top-flight college rowing teams begin their season with athletes who already know how to row. Not Navy. At best they get half a boat of athletes with prior rowing experience before they start the season. Yet every year Navy will have more than five boats of eights (that's forty rowers and five coxswains) competitively rowing. I remember thinking, *We're going to get crushed by Princeton,* our opponent in our first race of the season, still nine months away. I knew rowers at Princeton; I knew how good they were. I was so focused on our collective lack of rowing experience that I found myself not believing we would be competitive during the season. I was so excited to row and compete at the highest levels in college, yet here we were, trying to teach people the basics when I felt we should already be preparing our boats to race. It was easy to think our chances were close to zero when you watched my future teammates over the summer "catching crabs" (getting the oar stuck in the water and sometimes getting flung out of the boat as a result) and even missing a stroke or two (whiffing the oar through the air instead of pulling it through the water). In the beginning of the summer, the coach wouldn't even let me row. In his English accent, he cautioned me: "All-den, no need for you to row just yet. You'll only get your knickers in a knot." The first two months of my college rowing career were spent riding in the coach's launch (boat), watching my teammates learn to row.

Imagine being a D1 coach where 90 percent of your new athletes must be taught how to play the sport before they can compete. Is that a winning strategy against the best teams in the country? I wouldn't have thought so and certainly didn't believe it myself until we started racing—and winning. Before I tell you how Navy pulls off this miracle of coaching, let me give you a few other constraints that all service-academy coaches face. First, there are no redshirt years—all athletes must graduate in four years. Second, there are height and weight standards. Rowing favors tall people because height leads to length in the water, which means more distance for more speed, but Navy can't recruit the tallest kids because of height and weight restrictions on its ships and airplanes. Then there's the American citizen requirement; today many of the top college rowing programs recruit athletes from overseas. Some of these foreign athletes have already rowed on national teams and in the Olympics. Not the case with Navy's crew: all must be US citizens.

What's the secret to Navy's rowing prowess despite all these obstacles? The magic comes from the one thing that connects all students at the Naval Academy: our focus on serving. We have only four years to give it our all before serving our country. We have a different perspective than other college kids do. We can't take a semester off or a gap year to gain a competitive advantage. Our only advantage is our common bond to serve. We would never be the most experienced or tallest team in the race, but we would always be the crew with the biggest hearts.

Within a few months, I had witnessed my future teammates progress from rowing on a massive training barge, with coaches walking up and down the middle of this floating flattop boat patiently correcting each oarsman, to rowing with me in sleek twenty-four-inch-by-sixty-six-foot carbon-fiber rowing shells. When the summer started, I could easily beat their times on the stationary rowing machine called an ergometer, which measures pulling power, because I knew how to be more efficient on it. Yet within six months, many of my teammates were outpulling me. Their willingness to give it their all—to go all in—was remarkable and completely changed my perspective. Not only might we win some races, but I was learning firsthand what it took to build an unstoppable team. We all arrived at the Navy boathouse coming from different backgrounds, but we all left united with a single purpose. As different as we were, we all shared the will to serve. What's more, our diverse backgrounds and skills made us stronger together. Teammates who hadn't rowed before took different approaches to learning the sport. The brawny farm kids applied the same work ethic they'd grown up with. Their philosophy was simple: work harder than the competition. The former football and basketball players adapted training techniques from those sports to rowing. Athletes with an engineering background tended to take a more analytical approach by breaking down the mechanics of the rowing stroke to gain optimal force application. And then there were my pals from Texas who loved to remind us all in their Texas twang, "It ain't the size of the dog in the fight that matters; it's the size of the fight in the dog!" Good ol' Will Randall: technically he could have rowed lightweights (under 165 pounds) but he chose to race with us on the heavyweight squad. His attitude became our attitude as we embraced each Navy Crew racing season. (I later joined Will in SEAL Team. He served our country for over twenty years and today lives in Texas with his family.)

By the end of my freshman year, our boat had earned a bronze medal at the Eastern Championships and led the field by over a boat length for the National Championship with forty strokes left before an equipment malfunction (a seat broke) forced us to row across the finish line with six oarsmen. Even though we didn't win Nationals, here was a crew that included five oarsmen who had started rowing only eleven months ago but still finished fourth at the National Championship among twenty D1 collegiate teams. We had an astonishing record that season, and our success continued throughout my rowing career at Navy. I had expected our lack of experience to be our weakest link. Instead, I learned that inexperience can be overcome by relentless, committed team action.

Because of the diversity in our backgrounds, our experiences, and our approaches to training, we brought different superpowers to the effort, but our hearts were united. Ironically, I was the one who had the most negative thoughts bouncing around in my head at the start of the season. I was thinking, *How can we win against a crew that has all those top prep-school rowers?* My mind was focused on the superficial elements of a team, its pedigree. Yet my teammates would turn to me and say, "Millsy, those guys don't look that tough. This is going to be fun beating them." My own background as a rower—my ego—was my biggest obstacle to believing we could win. Everything changed after our first race. I came to understand why diversity was so important to teams, so long as the team shares a sense of purpose. We beat Princeton in that very first race.

After I graduated, when I became the leader of my BUD/S training class, I encountered even more diversity than at the Naval Academy. I watched classmates from landlocked states such as Oklahoma stare bug-eyed at a cresting six-foot wave. Some of my classmates had never seen waves that big, yet they would press on with some ranch-hand comment like "Damn, that there wave's taller than our John Deere combine." Then they'd put their heads down and paddle with all their might. Their will to keep going inspired me in much the same way my freshman teammates at Navy inspired me to pull harder. Watching my BUD/S classmates overcome their own fears made me dig deeper to do the same. Now, instead of pulling on oars, we were pulling for each other to pass physical tests, such as timed four-mile runs, obstacle courses, and two-mile ocean swims. Once again, here we were, a diverse group of people who might have different approaches to problems, but we all had a common commitment to the outcome. Our first rule was to keep going!

Abraham Lincoln set an example for leaders by cultivating diversity among his advisers as he faced the oncoming civil war. Imagine for a moment that you've worked tirelessly for your entire adult life to earn the opportunity to lead, but just as you assume your position, half of the people you are to lead leave. How incredibly discouraging that must have felt! What kind of team would you have assembled to help you lead during this unprecedented time in the history of the United States? Your instincts might have led you to surround yourself only with your allies, like-minded comrades.

It would be easy to rationalize filling your presidential Cabinet with friends who you knew had your political back. You could easily argue that trust beats experience as you assemble your team. However, by surrounding yourself with familiarity, you will inadvertently make yourself blind to other points of view. The most challenging team-building moments are when, like President Lincoln, you are forced to lead during divided times. We all know the outcome of the Civil War, but do you know how the sixteenth president built his team to tackle the greatest challenge to ever face any US president? He did what no other president before or since has done; he selected his top rivals to join his Cabinet, the very people who had done their best to prevent Lincoln from winning the election. He did so because he was intent on finding the best people, not on surrounding himself with his most loyal supporters. He placed a high value on diversity of thought. Though his rivals shared the same "heart"—they supported the abolition of slavery—each had very different opinions on how to make it a reality. President Lincoln embraced the discourse of difference to build a team that would help the nation meet its greatest challenges, from keeping it solvent during the war to crafting the laws that ended slavery. The president knew he could not conquer these monumental challenges alone and was willing to dampen his own ego and endure the egos of others who had the skills he needed to lead the nation back from the brink of self-destruction. Do you know what President Lincoln's superpower was? Sure, he was well read and had a penchant for working hard, but his true genius came from his ability to build relationships—to form teams that represented the diverse spectrum of thoughts and beliefs held by the American people. Historian Doris Kearns Goodwin, who wrote *Team of Rivals*, credits Lincoln with an uncommon ability to forge relationships through difference. Let President Lincoln's example be a lesson in team building. The better you are at forging relationships, especially with those who disagree with you, the more unstoppable you'll become as a team builder and leader.

I started this chapter with a focus on understanding what you are truly great at, so you can more easily push your ego aside and embrace different perspectives from others. No one person can do it all. The challenge is to overcome our self-centered thoughts and to willingly accept that other people can have better ideas. Having led all kinds of different teams in the last twenty-five years, from sports to SEALs to companies and charities, I have discovered seven traits that characterize unstoppable teammates. These are the general traits required—the must-haves for powerful team dynamics—regardless of the team's circumstances and challenges.

1. **COMPETENCE**—a curiosity to learn new skills and develop mastery of new subjects
2. **PERSPECTIVE**—thoughtfulness about the way past experiences and challenges have shaped attitudes, beliefs, and behavior
3. **COMMUNICATION**—the ability and willingness to express ideas and emotions

4. **DRIVE**—a can-do spirit, a strong work ethic, a hunger to succeed

5. **HUMILITY**—inclusiveness, self-awareness, and respect for others

6. **FLEXIBILITY**—an openness to new perspectives and the adaptability to let go of one idea or belief to embrace another

7. **SELFLESSNESS**—a willingness to serve others and to place the truth and others' interests above self-interest

Most team builders do not have the luxury of cherry-picking teammates from a broad pool of applicants. Leaders are usually thrust into situations where team members are inherited, not selected. No matter—great leaders learn to work with what they've got by finding out how to activate each person's best qualities on behalf of the team. The seven traits are those best qualities, and the more you demonstrate those qualities in your own actions, the more your teammates will learn to emulate them. After all, a team's personality and its actions are a direct reflection of its leader.

COMPETENCE

I use the word *competence* to define a cluster of intellectual skills. I'm not talking about book smarts or SAT scores or even your grades in high school or college. The skills I'm referring to are a person's willingness, capacity, and curiosity to learn new concepts and apply them to the right circumstances. Unstoppable teams are learning machines. As Heraclitus said, there is only one constant—change. It's a given that teammates must have the prerequisite mental capabilities to do the tasks required. After all, you wouldn't hire a software programmer to play the violin in an orchestra. But you do want to select team members as much for how they think as for what they can do, judged by how curious they are to discover and learn. The ability to learn, comprehend, and apply new concepts and techniques is critical for overcoming challenges. The most adept teams can apply lessons learned from other environments to solve challenges. Some people are more adept with words; others are more skilled with imagery and visual representation. Some people like to dive deep into the details; others synthesize patterns and see the big picture. Some people like to solve problems; others like to identify creative possibilities. Some people like to think first and then talk; others gain energy from relationships and brainstorming. There's no one right way to think or to learn or to approach problems. Indeed, your team is stronger if it can draw on all these approaches, and the competence of your team members will aid them in setting aside their egos to embrace different problem-solving approaches.

PERSPECTIVE

I use the term *perspective* because it reflects the way a person responds to life. Perspective comes from experience—how a person thinks and has responded to past challenges and obstacles. Were the challenges limiting to the person or were they inspiring? How did the person handle the hardship? How does he or she feel about facing the same obstacle again? The response will reveal that person's perspective.

Another way to think about it comes from Stanford psychologist Carol Dweck, whose research contrasts what she calls a fixed mind-set versus a growth mind-set. Those with fixed mind-sets tend to believe that physical, mental, or emotional talents, skills, and competencies are set in stone. Those with a growth mind-set, on the other hand, tend to believe that talents, skills, and competencies can be learned and improved through hard work, determination, and resilience. Professor Dweck labeled these mind-set traits back in 2006, but special-operations training throughout the United States military has been testing for these traits for well over fifty years—by training teams to develop tenacity, grit, and adaptability. From the Green Berets to SEAL Team, all special-forces units test candidates for their ability to push past their preconceived limit to succeed. People's perspective about hardship is a telling indicator of how they will perform on a team when encountering seemingly insurmountable obstacles.

COMMUNICATION

When I use the word *communication*, I don't mean you need to write like a bestselling author or speak like a great orator, but you do need the courage to communicate your ideas and your emotions. How people communicate is critical to team dynamics. (I will go into much more detail about this skill in chapter 3.) In much the same way that a stereo (or iPod) is only as good as the speakers the music is heard through, so it is with a person's ability to communicate. You can be the smartest or most creative person on the planet, but if you aren't able to communicate honestly, humbly, and persuasively, your contributions to the team will be limited. Likewise, if you lack the ability to modulate your emotions, you'll also be of limited use to a team, and your teammates will find it difficult to build a relationship with you. President Lincoln had a technique for preventing his emotions from sabotaging his communication; he kept a notepad filled with his thoughts and feelings before he spoke, which enabled him to manage his emotions without letting them interfere with or harm his communications with others. I don't expect everyone to employ a Lincolnesque communication methodology, but I do look closely at how people communicate with me, especially under stress or when dealing with a difficult subject or a conflict.

DRIVE

People can have all the skills and talents required to be great, but if they lack drive, then they are worse than useless to the team; they are dangerous in that they can infect other team members with mediocrity and negativity. That's why SEAL training has an "X division," which is where quitters are sent. SEAL candidates still slugging it out in the training arena aren't allowed to socialize with those who have decided to leave. Of course, in the civilian world, there's no X division, so leaders must be especially vigilant in rooting out any actions of the team that will negatively affect motivation and drive. Similarly, Sir Ernest Shackleton feared lack of drive more than anything else on his two-year journey to save his crew after losing his ship in the ice floes of Antarctica. At the first signs of any of his men losing heart, Shackleton commanded them to bunk with him, so he could restore their motivation to keep going. He viewed lack of drive as an enemy, and his actions proved the value of the saying "Keep your friends close and your enemies closer." People's hunger, their willingness to work hard—their drive—is critical to building healthy team dynamics. The value of this quality cannot be overstated. A leader can teach skills, but once the team's motivation starts to flag, you are in trouble.

HUMILITY

Humility is relatively easy to spot. Does a person spend all of his time bragging about how much he's accomplished, or does he discuss how others have helped him? Does she acknowledge her weaknesses or respond with "Gee, I can't think of any"? A favorite question of mine is asking people about their biggest failure. When you hear someone say, "I guess I've just been lucky, because I've never failed" or "I haven't failed but I've been around others who have," you know you're dealing with someone who doesn't get humility. Humble people listen twice as much as they speak; they speak of "we" and "us." They are quick to point out the accomplishments of others and can be critical of their own shortcomings. Jim Collins, author of *Good to Great*, considers humility a pinnacle trait of the best leaders. He's not alone in highlighting the value of humility. Patrick Lencioni, author of *The Ideal Team Player*, calls humility one of three must-haves for a team player (hunger and smarts are the other two). Humility is to a team as grease is to a machine; it enables all parts to function more smoothly and with less effort. Humility helps transition people from worrying about who is getting credit to focusing on how to get the job done. It is the quality that is most helpful in moving people from selfishness to the last critical quality of a team: selflessness.

To be sure, drive and humility don't always go hand in

hand. All too often, you run into people whose drive comes at any cost. They willingly sacrifice their personal integrity and relationships in service of their goals. They justify these lapses in judgment as "what it takes" to get ahead. In their quest for recognition, they never miss an opportunity to promote themselves at the expense of others. When they succeed, they tout their superlative skills as the cause of their success, yet when they stumble, they are quick to place blame on others. This me-first mentality is the exact opposite of the attitude you seek in teammates. It's humility, not hubris, that you're after. People with humility are grounded; they have the self-confidence of knowing their strengths and weaknesses and don't need to step on others to highlight their accomplishments. Nothing hurts team dynamics more than one person taking all the credit for the team effort. Conversely, it can be powerful when teammates, and especially the team leader, acknowledge individual contributions.

After my company was named one of *Inc.*'s fastest-growing companies in the country, reporters asked, "How did you invent the Perfect Pushup?" My response: "With twenty-five other people." On a much grander scale, when the four-star Navy SEAL admiral in command of the mission to kill Osama bin Laden was asked, "Who shot America's number-one terrorist?" his response was simple: "America shot him." He went on to explain how the American people enabled our military to reorganize, to train differently, and consequently to be better prepared when situations like these would arise. I love his answer because it's exactly how a team leader should be thinking—recognizing and praising the entire team.

FLEXIBILITY

The sixth quality to cultivate in unstoppable team members is flexibility—the ability to adjust one's mind-set as conditions change. Nothing ever goes as planned, and the way your team embraces those changes in real time determines the chances for success. I speak from experience. When I started my company, I wasn't as flexible as I should have been. If I had been paying attention to the sales data, really listening to what customers were telling me, I would have changed the direction of my product much sooner. I had the drive to succeed, but my lack of humility and flexibility caused me to dig in my heels until I was forced to change things four years later. I had raised $1.5 million to launch my product and ended up spending $1.475 million on what turned out to be the *wrong* ways to launch it—all because I didn't appreciate that flexibility was a strength, not a weakness. Only after I was facing personal bankruptcy did I change course and launch a different product (the Perfect Pushup). When people become set in their ways, they become blind to other opportunities. An attitude of flexibility keeps the leader's and the team's eyes open to spot changes on the horizon and make adaptability one of the team's superpowers.

One of the very few things we can control is our attitude, and you would be surprised how attitudes, from drive to humility to flexibility, can vary even at the highest levels of performance. My biggest leadership challenges in SEAL Team always stemmed from attitude. Having a careless attitude when wiring explosives or a reckless approach to patrolling an urban environment puts more than one person into unnecessary risk of major harm.

There are other attitudes that I had to deal with as well, such as complacency ("we're good enough") or even laziness ("we don't need to train harder"). These are negative attitudes that can block one's own potential and thus the team's potential.

SELFLESSNESS

Whether we're serving in the military, in a company, or in a nonprofit organization, we all have a choice about where we work and how much we want to give. Here's where selflessness comes in: understanding how much people are willing to give of themselves to the team. In SEAL Team, selflessness is the rule—"I've got your back," no matter what. SEALs go into work knowing that they might have to give the ultimate sacrifice, their lives, to get a mission done. That's an extreme commitment, and certainly not for everyone, but the same mentality exists in civilian life, albeit in a less dramatic form. Where do you think your team members will learn how to be open to other perspectives, to other ideas, to other points of view? From you, the team leader. How you serve your teammates will be the greatest predictor of how they will serve each other. You set the example; it's up to you to take the first steps of selfless action before others will follow your lead.

Some people are by nature more willing to give than others before receiving anything in return. Parents are especially attuned to this. Women surpass men four to one in production of oxytocin, the hormone that induces childbirth and lactation and promotes feelings of empathy in both sexes. Regardless of background, caring for others arouses our most powerful emotions; we are genetically programmed to respond to caring behavior. The teams you inherit may not show a natural proclivity or passion for serving, but by your actions of serving them—by showing that you care about their growth and well-being (see chapter 3)—you will catalyze the transformation of a group of loosely knit individuals into an unstoppable team.

Selflessness isn't just about serving others; it's also about serving the truth. It may sound odd to "serve the truth," but it's exactly what's required of you. Serving others and serving the truth go hand in hand. One cannot be trustworthy if one doesn't serve with honesty at all times. *Honor* may seem like an old-fashioned word, but it is more important than ever. Technology will change, weather patterns will change, political climates will change, but your selfless commitment to acting honorably and with integrity should never change. It is the bedrock on which all relationships are built. Maintaining one's honor, humility, and integrity is elemental in unstoppable teams.

People are not one-dimensional. We all have aptitudes and attitudes, and what we do with them defines us. No one person can do it all. Each of us has a gift—a superpower—that when practiced and honed can be an important component of the team we serve. The biggest obstacle to personal and team success is the ego. It can lull us into thinking we are better than we are, it can block us from accepting better ideas, and it can turn away the very people who could help us succeed. In building a team, a team leader's first order of business is understanding her strengths and weaknesses. The better a leader knows herself, the more readily she can surround herself with people who possess complementary strengths and perspectives.

Remember that we can control only three things: our mental, emotional, and physical capabilities. What we focus on drives how we behave, which determines what we do. This process for individual action is the same for team actions. Your job as team builder and leader is to develop a team that embodies these seven traits, to direct the team's focus, and to set an example of the behaviors that will drive the actions required to succeed. How well people embrace the focus and behaviors that you prioritize will have a direct impact on the actions taken. As you scale from a team of one (leading your action platform) to a team of many, your greatest challenge is to *connect* with them, the first step in activating the CARE framework.

C.A.R.E. Loop

CHAPTER 3

CONNECT

Dad converted our beige Buick station wagon into a make-shift ambulance with pillows and a blanket from the pullout sofa that had been my bed for the last two weeks. It was the second time I had been diagnosed with pneumonia, but this time was different. Every time I turned to one side, I saw flashes of white light that triggered jolts of pain in my back. It was late at night, so Dad took me to the hospital while Mom stayed home with my younger brother. When I arrived, the doctors feared I had spinal meningitis and rushed me into a solitary area for a spinal tap. Until that moment at the age of twelve, the two most uncomfortable experiences in my life had been the time I flipped over the handlebars of my bicycle (eleven stitches to the forehead) and the time I impaled my right thigh on an oarlock as I fell off a dock onto a rowboat at low tide. Having spinal fluid sucked from between my vertebrae was much worse.

A spinal tap requires a steady hand by the doctor inserting the needle and a very still fetal-positioned patient. It's a delicate procedure that can have dire consequences for the patient if the doctor damages any of the nerves in the spinal cord. I didn't quite understand why there were so many people gathered in the room until the needle entered my back. Two nurses, each holding a bedpan, took their positions, one near my head and the other near my backside. My father held my head while another nurse pinned my hips to the bed. It was a good thing everyone was there, because I needed all of them. I never thought one could vomit and defecate at the same time (a mortally embarrassing experience for me, as I was just entering puberty and both bedpan-wielding nurses were female).

Thankfully, the tests proved that I didn't have spinal meningitis, but the scare prompted my parents to seek out a pulmonary specialist. The pulmonologist was in Worcester, the largest city close to our small town of Southbridge, Massachusetts. His office was more like a laboratory than an examining room. He had me perform a series of tests, from blowing into machines to timing how long I could keep a Ping-Pong ball afloat between a couple of lines inside a tube. Each breathing exercise received a numerical value and was charted on a graph. After about a half hour of various tests, he put one hand up and said, "That's enough. I understand the issue."

He ushered my mother and me over to a table in the middle of his laboratory, held up the graph he had plotted with my results, turned to my mother, and said, "Mrs. Mills, it is obvious what is wrong with your son. You see this graph"—he pointed to a series of dots—"this is your son's approximate lung capacity, and this is a normal child's lung capacity for his age." He paused for a moment and then added, "Your son has a smaller-than-average set of lungs for his size and has asthma." Again he paused before offering his recommendation: "I can prescribe medication for his asthma, but I suggest he lead a less active lifestyle and learn the game of chess."

I heard the word *chess* and my chin dropped to my chest. Mom sensed my disappointment, tapped me on the shoulder, and asked me to go to the waiting room while she spoke to the lung doctor. By the time Mom returned to the reception area, tears were streaming down my face. Mom looked at me for a moment and then asked, "Alden, what's wrong with you? Why are you crying?"

I looked up at her and exclaimed, "Mom! Chess? I'm not any good at *checkers*!"

She knelt down in front of me, grabbed my left forearm with her right hand, and dug her long fingernails into my arm. "You listen to me. No one, and I mean *no one*"—her nails dug deeper into my skin—"defines what you can or can't do. That's up to you. Now I'll get you the medicine, but you decide what you can do. Do you hear me?"

At first it was hard not to fixate on what the doctor had said. Every time I found myself short of breath, I'd think, *Better slow down* or *Time for the inhaler—asthma kicking in.* It was easy to feel sorry for myself or make excuses for why I didn't run as fast as someone else—and even easier to justify why I shouldn't push myself. My brain was great at replaying the scene from when the doctor said, "Your son has a smaller-than-average set of lungs...has asthma...I suggest he lead a less active lifestyle." But over time, that movie got replaced by other scenes, punctuated by my mother's words: "You decide what you can do." The first test of that statement came when I tried out for the high school rowing club.

I can still remember the first time I watched the sport of rowing. I was a passenger in the very same station wagon that had been my makeshift ambulance a couple of years earlier. We drove around a bend in the road that bordered the Housatonic River. Three sleek, white fiberglass rowing shells gleamed in the water. I was mesmerized by the perfection of eight oars all striking the water at the same time; it looked like a giant centipede gliding over the water. I immediately felt a connection with the sport. For starters, I loved the idea of sitting down versus running! Not to mention a sport involving boats with the sole purpose of going fast on the water. It represented perfect teamwork to me—no top scorers, no

MVPs—just eight athletes pulling their oars in synchronicity. My desire to be good at this sport overrode the voice I'd been hearing in my head after the lung doc's diagnosis. Instead, I started paying attention to the encouraging words my parents had been giving voice to over the past two years: *That's up to you.* One success led to another and another, and over time I built the confidence to try greater physical pursuits. Rowing took me to the Naval Academy, then to SEAL Team, and eventually to starting my first business. (Starting a business might not seem physically demanding, but trust me: stress is stress, and that makes it physical.)

I shudder to think what my life would be like today if I hadn't listened to my parents but instead had embraced the suggestions of that doctor. I wish him no ill will; he was only trying to keep me safe by reducing my exposure to sickness. And in part he was correct, because I did get sick again and again, and sometimes at the worst times. I made the varsity crew in high school but then was removed because I contracted pneumonia. I encountered more lung infections at the Naval Academy, missing days of rowing practice. My Navy teammates would apply their sense of humor to my absences by taping a marshmallow to my seat and rowing the boat without me using only seven instead of eight rowers for the practice; and then they would tell the coach (in front of me) that the marshmallow made them faster than I did! The worst lung infection occurred during SEAL training and forced me to be rolled back a class and repeat weeks of the second phase of training. None of those experiences were particularly enjoyable, but by then each illness was familiar to me; it didn't deter me from accomplishing my goal. My parents—through their straightforward communication, the consistency of their love and support, and their commitment to my well-being and my personal growth—gave me the support and encouragement I needed to press on and harden my resolve.

The reason I have shared this story with you is that it demonstrates the power of connection and, ultimately, the power of trust. And yes, love. No matter what industry you work in or what position you hold, your success depends on your ability to build human relationships. At the center of relationship building is empathy—the ability to place yourself in your colleagues' shoes, to understand their point of view or, more important, their feelings. Building connections with others requires empathy, and empathizing requires that you show vulnerability and act with transparency.

If what I'm describing sounds a lot like the role that parents play in a child's life, that's not a mistake. My mother also suffered from asthma, and she would often share her experiences with me about how she'd learned to manage the ailment. I kept trying new things because I trusted her more than anyone, even a doctor who was an expert in pulmonary disorders. That's the same kind of trust you'll find in unstoppable teams. It's the kind of connection you'll need to build with your team to achieve greatness. We all have doubts about our own capabilities, but when someone we trust encourages us to persist despite our fears and reservations, we can accomplish more than we originally thought was possible.

It may seem unrealistic to expect great teams to employ the same tactics that my mom used to carry me forward, but actually they do. It's this level of care that makes some teams unstoppable and others just mediocre. Unfortunately, some people haven't had the benefit of positive experiences with their parents. They may have developed coping mechanisms to compensate for the love, safety, and support they didn't receive at home. Insecurities abound from all kinds of past experiences. One of your primary jobs as a care-based team builder is to learn how to connect using all three forms of human connection—physical, mental, and emotional—in order to break through people's defenses, those psychological barriers they've erected to protect themselves from getting hurt. As "touchy-feely" as this might sound, the highest-performing teams are built on a foundation of care, the same bedrock emotions that keep families healthy and happy. As President Abraham Lincoln said, "In order to win a man to your cause, you must first reach his heart, the great high road to his reason," and that's exactly what this chapter is about: winning people over by connecting with their hearts.

In the pages that follow, I'll introduce techniques to help you establish trust with different types of people. But before I go further, I want you to understand why it is so critically important to connect with people. And remember, when I use the term *connect*, I'm not talking about sending an e-mail; I'm talking about building the bonds of human relationships, engaging people at the deepest levels, both mentally and emotionally. If you're still skeptical about the value of these kinds of deep connection, consider this troubling finding from a Gallup survey, "US Employee Engagement": nearly two-thirds of the US workforce isn't engaged at work.

But that's not all. Gallup reports that 16 percent of employees are actively *disengaged* at work and only 21 percent report feeling fully engaged. On the flip side, almost 60 percent of employees who are led by engaged leaders report being engaged and motivated at work.[1] This report paints a bleak picture of US corporate leadership. It shows the need for more emphasis on the "soft" aspects of leadership that I address in the CARE framework. According to Gallup's findings, only four out of ten people feel cared for at work. That lack undoubtedly affects workers' attitude and performance, not to mention their physical health. They may be "present" at the job, but they are not engaged, and they are anything but unstoppable.

Where does engagement start? Do you think it begins

when you're reviewing someone's work? Or perhaps when you give people a deadline or lay out the specifics of a task? Engagement isn't a start-and-stop process, a checklist to be completed. It needs constant attention, and it begins and ends (and begins again, on and on) with knowing each of your teammates as an individual.

Johnson & Johnson had been named as one of the most admired companies in the United States for sixteen years in a row by *Fortune* magazine. When I was getting my MBA, I interned at J&J's headquarters for a summer. It was my first civilian job after SEAL Team, and I was thrilled to be selected for the opportunity. I had read Jim Collins and Jerry Porras's *Built to Last* and was impressed by their research connecting mission statements with company performance. At the top of their list was J&J's credo, four paragraphs on the purpose and business philosophy of the pharmaceutical company. As the authors noted, mission statements don't automatically make companies successful, but they can drive superior performance if they're put into practice.

I remember my excitement on the first day at J&J, thinking, *I'm going to get firsthand experience learning from the best about mission statements!* Mission statements had been a big deal to me in SEAL Team. By the time I led my third platoon, I ran a process for my teammates to create our own platoon mission statement: Combat ready for mission success anytime, anywhere. It wasn't fancy, but it was ours; we had made it together and committed ourselves to it. We even had it carved into a small brass plaque and attached to our platoon log. Not a log*book*—no, we had a four-foot wooden log that went everywhere our platoon headquarters went. We would position it in our office as the first and last thing we'd see when entering and exiting for training or a mission.

J&J didn't disappoint me. The first four hours of my first day were spent with other new hires—interns, part-timers, and full-timers—learning how to connect with the credo. In the beginning, the class wasn't particularly inspiring. We were each handed a single sheet of paper with the credo typed on it and were asked to read it quietly to ourselves.

It begins, "We believe our first responsibility is to the doctors and the nurses, to mothers and fathers and all others who use our products and services." The four paragraphs explicitly state that the company's priorities are customers, employees, community, and shareholders—in that order. It is rare to see profitability to investors ranked last in such a list. Nevertheless, it was what the instructor said next that really struck me: "I would like you all to think of a time when someone you cared for deeply used one or more J&J products." The company has lots of products, but perhaps its best-known is Band-Aids. My mind started racing through moments when I had used Band-Aids—the time, for instance, when I'd thrown a rock at my brother's head and split the skin wide open. I remember how awful I'd felt moments later as my mother applied J&J bandages to stop the bleeding. The instructor asked each of us to reflect on those memories and then asked us to relate our story to the rest of the group. One by one, we shared a story and then discussed our feelings. I didn't realize it at the time, but this process helped each of us, and the group collectively, form an emotional connection to the company's credo and to each other. The credo came alive that day because we weren't just intellectually connected; we were becoming emotionally and, as you will see later in this chapter, physically bonded to each other. Individual experiences will differ, of course, but if we can connect our memories with a shared purpose, we are well on the way to becoming unstoppable.

Connecting with people requires using all three components of your action platform: your mental, emotional, and physical capabilities to prove to others you are trustworthy. What does it mean to deeply connect with others? It means you must bring curiosity, authenticity, and candor, a willingness to listen, and above all else a consistency to your intent to build connections. You need to connect and collaborate with your team members—to understand their worries, fears, and perceived limitations and then collaborate with them to overcome challenges. Each challenge that is overcome deepens your connections to each other and increases your confidence to take on even more difficult goals.

Remember, though: just because you're the designated leader doesn't mean that you'll find it easy to earn your team's trust. As a leader, you don't have an automatic, innate connection. You must build it through what I call the three Cs:

1. **COMMUNICATION**—physical, mental, emotional
2. **CREDIBILITY**—integrity, accountability, humility
3. **COMMITMENT**—reliability, consistency, focus

Don't think of these as a sequence of events but rather a matrix of interwoven actions that gradually forge trusting relationships. They all interact with one another. Your body language must match your words, and your words must be consistent with your intent. All these factors come together, sometimes subtly and sometimes overtly, to convey your authenticity and trustworthiness. The three Cs are a package deal; they build upon and reinforce each other, and you can't have one without practicing all of them.

COMMUNICATION

I chose the fitness industry to start my first business in part because I'd always had a personal passion for it. Exercise was (and is) a key contributor to helping me overcome my medical maladies and achieve my educational and professional goals. When I think of exercise, I think of transformation; I think of overcoming obstacles and building stamina to achieve more than I originally thought possible. The connection I have with fitness is personal and powerful. But that's not the case for most people. For many, the words *fitness* and *exercise* conjure up images of sweaty gyms, bodybuilders, and lots of hard work. Most don't have a positive image of fitness, so when it came time to recruit top talent to build my team, I struggled to find people who shared my connection and commitment to a life of fitness. It took me several years to understand how to tailor my message to connect with potential "internal" teammates, but also with "external" teammates—those whom most businesspeople would simply call customers. (I will address this mind shift in chapter 7, but suffice it to say here that, for me, customers are also teammates.) If you can't form a connection with the talented people you're trying to recruit to your team, how will you ever connect with your customers? Sure, you might get them for one purchase, but that's not sustainable nor desirable for the long term. Your future teammates, whether they are called employees, customers, volunteers, sailors, or soldiers, need to feel a connection before they will commit their time, money, and energy. The first way you connect with others is through communication.

You might think that's obvious, but do you know that 55 percent of face-to-face communication occurs without even muttering a word? That's right: studies have proven that most of our communication comes through body language and tone. Thirty-eight percent is how we say it, and only 7 percent is what we say. Before you dismiss this study as some half-baked academic research that doesn't apply to the real world, think about what you learn from someone's body posture. Here are some examples to get your mind going:

1. Slouching in chair
2. Shuffling feet
3. Chin on the chest
4. Drooping shoulders
5. Hunching forward

The list could go on, but you know these positions and more. Each one of these postures communicates something negative about the person who is assuming them—from "I don't care" to "not interested" to "no energy" to "I'm defeated and don't think it's possible." People may be saying the opposite, but their body language doesn't lie; indeed, it communicates a message more powerful than words. Most of the time, we have already formed an impression of other people before they even open their mouths.

Now add facial expressions and eye contact. We have forty-three muscles in our face that can create twenty-one expressions, representing everything from sadness to glee. Then there's eye contact. Looking people in the eyes—as opposed to looking at their feet, above their heads, or at your hands—communicates volumes before you even open your mouth. Learn to use all these elements of body posture, facial expression, and eye contact in synergy and with intent, and you'll find that your ability to connect and to build trust increases.

Have you ever spoken to someone who didn't turn to face you? What did that make you feel like? Do you think that person was committed to you or cared about you and the points you were trying to make? Let's say you're sitting at your desk and someone comes over to ask you for help. Are you inclined to say yes if that person takes a knee to be at your eye level (or, even better, below your eye level) and makes direct eye contact? That action communicates loudly. Few of us would be able to resist stopping what we're doing, turning to the person, and listening with the intent of understanding how we might help. Which of these two scenarios makes you feel more connected with someone when you walk into that person's office?

a. You walk in, but the person doesn't look up from the computer screen or shift posture to acknowledge your presence.

b. You walk in and, as you do, the person turns from the computer screen to you, makes immediate eye contact, stands, and comes to greet you.

Assuming you've already been given permission to enter the person's office space, A and B are both wordless communications. Both set the tone for what kind of connecting happens next. In scenario A, you aren't thinking of connecting; you don't even think that person cares about you. Your defenses go up, your mind goes into fight-or-flight or even freeze mode. The only issue you're thinking about now is how soon you can leave. In scenario B, body language communicates something entirely different. You don't feel threatened; you relax, and your mind remains open to thinking creatively. The first example conveys how *not* to connect, while the second demonstrates the basics of connecting with care.

Now layer in the mental components of communicating. Are you preoccupied by your own thoughts and your own needs? When you speak, do you use *I* and *me* a lot? Do you say that people work *for* you or *with* you? Do you address people using your authority: "I need you to do *x* by *y* time"? Or do you ask for help or advice before discussing getting a task done? We all know people who use their status or position of power as if it grants them the right to boss people around. They think leadership is telling people what to do. They don't build trust; they create micromanagers who fear them, and then they wonder why their division doesn't hit the numbers or create world-beating products. News flash! Time, money, and inventory get managed; processes and projects need to be managed too. But not *people*. They want to be seen for who they are; they want to be recognized for their superpowers; they want to contribute; they want to be led, liked, and, yes, even loved. We all seek love and opportunities to learn and contribute, and we need to feel connection, not just to other people but to the purpose of our work, too. That's what Gallup's research calls engagement. That's what I mean by connection. It's not a "nice-to-have"; it's a fundamental human need. We want to know you care about us as individuals, not as machines or tools to achieve your goals. As the Gallup survey authors put it, "Employees need to know that someone is concerned about them as people first and as employees second." On unstoppable teams, employees are teammates. They don't serve their leader; their leader serves them, and in turn they serve each other and the team's purpose. When you open your mouth, choose your words wisely and give people some context for understanding why they should align themselves with you. As the team leader, *you* are the first and best person to give them a reason to believe that what they're doing matters.

One of the most successful basketball coaches in NCAA history is Mike Krzyzewski, aka Coach K. His teams have won back-to-back NCAA championships and participated in seven Final Four championships. He is the all-time winningest college basketball coach, having recently passed Pat Summitt of Tennessee. Coach K's book, *Leading with the*

Heart, outlines his coaching philosophy. Authentic communication is at the heart of his approach: "People are not going to follow you as a leader unless you show them that you're real. They are not going to believe you unless they trust you. And they are not going to trust you unless you always tell them the truth and admit when you were wrong."[2]

It doesn't matter whether you're coaching basketball teams, leading SEAL Teams, or building corporate teams; all teams are built on relationships. A team builder's role is to be a relationship builder, which requires learning how to connect with people mentally and emotionally.

The third component of effective communication is using feelings as a powerful tool for connecting with others. For example, when it comes to collaboration, all too many leaders start with the good intentions of seeking someone's advice on an issue, only to mess it up by being insincere. At the heart of connecting emotionally with others is curiosity. The hunger to learn from others comes from being curious—curious about others' backgrounds and points of view and curious about different approaches to solving a challenge. In team building, the adage "Curiosity killed the cat" doesn't apply; instead the team motto is "Curiosity connects."

Starting from a point of curiosity (and thus vulnerability), rather than certainty, sets the tone for how you collaborate with others. If you don't know how to collaborate and leverage your team's superpowers, you're bound to hit obstacles. But if you embrace the three core actions at the heart of every successful collaboration—asking, listening, and understanding—you'll draw strength and resources from everyone. Collaborating is hard because it requires you to acknowledge that you—the person of authority—don't know everything. By collaborating, you are acknowledging that you need others' help, that you know they're better at something than you are, and that their ideas matter and provide value to the team. To start off on the right foot, ask questions that start with a statement: "We need your help solving this problem." You're communicating that their ideas matter, that you care, and that you are bound together emotionally in the quest to find solutions and breakthrough ideas.

Step two is where many people make a mistake: they don't know how to listen. We've all experienced a situation where our opinion is solicited but not really valued. It's easy to spot those pretending to listen; they don't maintain eye contact, or they may be distracted by other tasks, such as checking e-mail or looking at a report. Body language and tone say, "I don't care about your opinion." They are likely to cross their arms (a closed position—i.e., not actively listening) and shift their weight onto their heels (i.e., disconnecting by not leaning into the conversation). This is not helpful; it is disingenuous and rude.

Selective listening is another trick people sometimes use. They aren't focused on your input, but rather on how they can rebut your opinion and prove you wrong. If you frequently find yourself interrupting others before they can answer your question or mentally preparing your response before the other person has completed a sentence, you are engaging in selective listening, which causes people to shut down and distrust you.

Active listening is listening with the intent to understand. You can spot an active listener by eye contact, gestures, and posture. The best active listeners give you their full attention; they ask follow-up questions to be sure they understand your points, they might take notes, and they use candor to build rapport. When people are relaxed—when they feel safe to express themselves, when they trust their teammates and their team leader—they are more creative. Active listeners may not agree with you and may not follow your suggestions, but they do show respect for you and sincerely value your input.

How you listen and respond determines whether you'll energize your team or cause them to disengage. Recent research from psychologists Naomi Eisenberger and George Kohlrieser shows that "feeling connected is intrinsically rewarding to the brain."[3] Put another way, true human connections feel good physically, and when people feel good, they tend to do good work. Conversely, when human connections suddenly split apart, our brains interpret this breakdown as physical pain. Dr. Eisenberger has found a physical correlation to the folkloric notion of a broken heart. We're wired to seek human connection, and the breakdown of those connections causes physical harm. Building connections with people isn't just good for team dynamics; it's good for everyone mentally, emotionally, *and* physically.

CREDIBILITY

Leaders live or die by their reputations. Your reputation or personal brand is nothing less than a promise, which is supported by people and a process. A person's brand promise is dependent not only on how they communicate but, equally important, on whether they are reliable, act with integrity, and hold themselves accountable for their actions. How you handle the truth or difficult situations, how you take ownership for your team's actions, and whether you follow through on your commitments determine your credibility. Ed Catmull, the cofounder and former president of Pixar and author of *Creativity, Inc.,* describes building credibility with teammates like this: "You need to show your people that you meant it when you said that while efficiency was *a* goal, quality was *the* goal. More and more, I saw that by putting people first—not just *saying* that we did but *proving* that we did by the actions we took—we were protecting that culture."

Whether you're a seasoned leader or an inexperienced

one, you must earn your credibility every day by consistent and committed action.

As I mentioned in chapter 1, the first thing you're taught when you enter the United States Naval Academy is how to stand. Soon after, you are instructed in how to respond. Freshmen at the Academy are called plebes, and as a plebe you learn the five basic responses to upperclassmen. They are:

"Yes, Sir/Ma'am."

"No, Sir/Ma'am."

"Aye, aye, Sir/Ma'am."

"I'll find out, Sir/Ma'am."

"No excuse, Sir/Ma'am."

Plebes learn these basic responses because Academy leadership is seeking to form a habit of accountability from day one. As part of their leadership training, upperclassmen take responsibility to teach underclassmen to be responsible for their actions. The first three responses are simple in their meaning. The final two are the important ones. "I'll find out" is meant to eliminate your natural inclination to BS your way through a situation. In the military, if you are not sure about something, leaders want you to admit it up front; otherwise someone could get hurt. For example, life on a submarine is exacting. You must know what happens when you turn a valve. Ignorance could have disastrous consequences, like the time a young enlisted man turned the wrong valve, sending eighty gallons of raw sewage down a ventilation shaft into our sleeping quarters. This mistake resulted in a six-hour emergency that kept the submarine on the surface, putting the entire crew at risk. This occurred because the young man—it was his first day on board—was scared to admit that he didn't know for sure what valve 41 did. The phrase "I'll find out" signals that you know it's OK not to know everything but that you accept the responsibility to figure out what you don't know. That builds credibility with your team.

The final response—"No excuse"—is all about accepting that the buck stops with you. If you didn't get something done, it's no one's fault but your own. It's the next step in taking responsibility for your actions and not placing blame on someone else. It's a hard one to stomach at first, especially when a classmate in your squad made the mistake that you are being held accountable for. Sometimes instructors purposefully put you in the position of accepting responsibility for something you didn't do. For example, during Plebe Summer, an instructor might remove one of three roommates from their quarters, make the remaining two prepare the room for inspection in a ridiculously short time, and then fail you because you didn't get the task done. Your first instinct might be to blame the missing roommate, but by forcing you into using one of the five basic responses, you are left with no other reply than "No excuse, Sir." As unfair as it may seem that you and your other roommate had to clean the missing roommate's side of the room, the fact is that the room is your responsibility with or without all roommates present. The situation isn't that different from what happens in a business organization or on the sports field. A shipmate may be on leave, a company colleague may be sick, or a teammate may be out of position. Still it's up to the team to fill the void. It's the hardest of the five basic responses to learn because you must take responsibility for other people's actions. You are not allowed to place blame on others. It is an important shift in mind-set that requires you to look out for others, not just yourself.

Now change the environment from being a plebe to starting your first company and reporting bad news to your investors. Imagine that you're one of those investors and you're asking the CEO, the leader of the company, "Why hasn't the product launched yet?" or "What happened in the first quarter?" Using the five basic responses wouldn't work here because more information is needed, but the spirit of "I'll find out" and "No excuse" is still an important element of your response. For example, how do you explain that the product hasn't launched yet? If you start by pointing fingers at everyone else but don't call out your own mistakes, then you lose credibility. However, if you start by owning the reasons why the product hasn't launched, then you can build more credibility with your investors—so long as you don't keep repeating the same mistakes again and again. That won't help your credibility either.

Sometimes credibility is lost or gained depending on how you answer the question, "What happened?" When calling out accomplishments and goals met, do you credit yourself or the people on your team who helped make it happen? On the flip side, when mistakes are made or goals are not fulfilled, do you take ownership for them or look to blame someone else? This is your "No excuse" moment. Pass the compliments around, but point the criticism at yourself. You may say that doesn't sound fair because "Bob blew it and ordered too much product," but it's your fault for not verifying Bob's order or creating a process to double-check inventory levels. By being quick to praise others for successes and to accept responsibility for failures, you aren't just building credibility; you are also acting with humility and integrity.

At the Naval Academy, integrity was simply defined: "Do not lie, cheat, or steal." These may seem like obvious rules to follow, but all too many leaders convince themselves that stretching the truth or avoiding bad news is justified. To the contrary, bad news must be voiced early and often. Likewise, your credibility will also be fortified when you take in different points of view that are directly in conflict with yours. Here again, how you listen matters. I know because I've done it the wrong way and then eventually the right way. In many cases when I've failed, the failure has occurred because my ego got in the way of listening to different points of view and truly understanding the potential outcomes. In two different instances, my failure to candidly communicate the good and bad news to investors cost me precious credibility—and almost my company.

The consequences of poor communication and selective listening can be even greater when you have the power to send people into battle, as was the case with Winston Churchill in World War I. Most are familiar with Prime Minister Churchill's extraordinary leadership during World War II, but that triumph was preceded by a failure so great that, years later, Churchill's wife, Clementine, told a biographer that she worried that her husband "would die from grief" dealing with the burden from his poor decision. His greatest leadership failure occurred while he was the lord of the Admiralty (secretary of the Navy) and had convinced Britain's War Cabinet to attack Turkey on a section of its coastline called Gallipoli. More than a million men fought for almost nine months, resulting in a half million casualties in all and a crushing defeat for the British Empire.

At the heart of this decision was the great orator's unwillingness to communicate (and listen to) different points of view. He became so fiercely attached to his point of view that he not only didn't listen to those around him, including Lord Admiral Fisher, head of the Royal Navy, who told him it was a "doomed plan," but he also distorted vital data when briefing the War Cabinet. He took aggressive steps to squelch those who opposed his plan of attack, even barring some dissenters from reaching the War Cabinet decision makers. His arrogance and unwillingness to embrace dissent and difference cost the lives of tens of thousands of British, Australian, and New Zealand soldiers.

Years later, Prime Minister Churchill implemented lessons learned from his disastrous Gallipoli decision when he was assembling his War Cabinet at the start of World War II. Like President Lincoln, he chose to embrace his rivals to ensure that communication would be truly open, candid, and subject to lively debate. Prime Minister Churchill is considered a great leader as much for how he learned from his mistakes as he is for his great successes. Righting our wrongs, responding to our shortcomings, and acknowledging our errors are essential in building credibility with others. If you do these actions well, people will come to trust you even more; if poorly or not at all, people's faith in you may be permanently eroded.

COMMITMENT

At SEAL Team Two, the command master chief (the senior enlisted petty officer of the team) would stand by the front door on Monday mornings to inspect haircuts. Technically speaking, I outranked him, but I was nowhere near his level of experience in SEAL Team. He had fifteen more years of service in the Teams than I. When he "suggested" that I needed to get a haircut that day, I listened. Having just returned from my trimming, I went into his office to show him my latest haircut. He smiled and asked, "Sir, do you know why I check everyone's haircut every Monday?" I didn't really know the answer, so I responded jokingly. "Because you like Marines, Master Chief!" (Marines keep their hair very short, as in bald on the sides.) He didn't laugh; instead he responded with one word: "Consistency." His reasoning was simple. Haircuts and even hairstyles are a sign of someone's brand. The more consistent you are in your actions, the more you are trusted, because people know what to expect. When your actions are inconsistent, you leave people guessing about your intentions. SEAL Team Two's command master chief didn't limit his inspections to haircuts; he was constantly checking our uniforms and gear lockers, even inspecting us before we left for deployments. To him, consistency was a habit, and it wasn't reserved for just part-time use. A professional should be consistent in all he or she does.

His attitude toward consistency resonated with me. No wonder—Naval Academy training was four years of learning to be consistent in our actions, our decorum, and our rooms (my hardest area to be consistent). If you're erratic in your actions, people don't know who you are. Inconsistent actions throw people off balance, and when they're wondering "what's next," they're spending more time guessing what the leader is going to do than focusing on what they should be doing to help the team. I'm not suggesting that you need to wear a uniform to work, like blue jeans and sneakers or Steve Jobs's black mock turtleneck, or that you should keep the same hairstyle for thirty-plus years (though it works for me), but I am pointing out that consistency in your actions and your behavior does cement trust with your teammates.

Think about this for a moment: if you say you're going to send weekly e-mail updates to your teammates but then stop abruptly or decide that it's not a big deal if you skip one or two because you're too busy, what message are you sending to your team? You are communicating complacency, not consistency. You're saying it's OK not to keep your commitments, because your team leader doesn't. When the world is crumbling around you and you have no idea what to do, your best tactic is to stay consistent. I've had times when I didn't know what to do, but I remained consistent, accepted accountability, and above all kept communicating. Sure, there were times when I wasn't as consistent as I should have been; it's the commitment to keep trying that counts.

We all develop our own styles of connecting, but the building blocks remain the same. No matter how we use our physical, mental, and emotional communication skills to connect with people, communication is a powerful way to build trust and create the caring conditions you want your teammates to emulate. The details matter, from how you listen to how you deal with bad news. If you yell and scream when something goes wrong, two things happen: others will yell and scream when they are delivered bad news; even worse, many won't even risk delivering bad news for fear of your yelling and screaming. That's a recipe for disaster. Connecting with your team is rewarding in its own right, for humans thrive on connections with others, but it's essential if you want to accomplish what I call an OTH goal—an over-the-horizon goal. Those kinds of goals are the most challenging because they are unknown, and our brains don't like the unknown. However, OTH goals are exactly the type that unstoppable teams can tackle. As you prepare to tackle OTH goals in your own work, pick elements from the three Cs that you can incorporate into your daily life. You probably do some of these actions already, but don't try to do too much at once. Remember, connecting with all kinds of people is a process of trial and error, and your leadership limits are determined by the diversity of personalities whom you can connect with. Don't despair if you don't get everything right at first; your commitment to keep trying will also earn you trust.

C.A.R.E. Loop

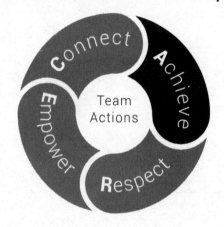

CHAPTER 4

ACHIEVE

Teams exist for one reason: to achieve results. So many people confuse a group, a club, or a gathering of people with a fully realized team. However, getting a group of people together is only the first step in the process (as discussed in chapter 2). Forming connections comes next (as discussed in chapter 3), and now we turn to the next step, which is setting the team's direction. Sometimes teams come together only briefly—to fight a fire, for instance, or to stabilize a patient in an emergency room. In other instances, teams are assembled to achieve a goal that requires years of sustained effort—whether it's a team of Pixar animators making a movie or a team of General Electric engineers implementing Six Sigma programs to eliminate defects in the manufacturing of jet engines. Unstoppable teams exist in all environments of crisis, creativity, and productivity, and they

all strive to achieve goals where the outcome is uncertain—
over-the-horizon goals that lie beyond our visibility and
push us out of our comfort zone. OTH goals stretch into
the unknown and often trigger a response of self-doubt. I
liken these types of goals, where the outcome is unknown,
to a person trying to navigate a small boat across an ocean—
that is, a goal characterized largely by what we can't see and
cannot know in advance. How far do you think a six-foot-
tall person can see if standing on top of a calm sea? I've put
this question before audiences all over the world, and they
are always surprised at the answer. It's not nearly as far as
you think: a mere 2.9 miles (without binoculars) before the
curvature of the earth curtails your field of view. Goals that
appear within our line of sight are the most comforting to us
because our brains crave certainty. But the goals that most
unstoppable teams aspire to reach exist beyond the line of
sight of any one individual. The team leader's role is to help
team members see well beyond the visible horizon and find
ways to surpass real and/or imagined limitations. I refer
to the team leader's actions as the five A's of Achievement:
Aspire, Assume, Assess, Assure, and Appreciate. Taken together, these five actions form the second part of the CARE
loop. Here's how I define each of them:

- **ASPIRE.** Bring the goal to life by helping team members
  personally connect to it. Give them hope and a reason

to believe that their collective efforts can achieve the task.

- **ASSUME.** Give your team the space, resources, and confidence to do their jobs.
- **ASSESS.** Initiate performance assessments frequently and transparently to avoid surprises and unify the team.
- **ASSURE.** Encourage and reassure your team of their purpose, progress, and perspective; help team members overcome their fears and doubts.
- **APPRECIATE.** Show enthusiasm and gratitude for both individual efforts and team progress.

ASPIRE

The seeds of this action begin when you form your team and connect with them emotionally, but aspirations need to be reinforced again and again. Your call to action inspires them to press on when achievement seems unlikely. You don't need to be a great orator like Winston Churchill, but you do need to be authentic in articulating a reason why people should believe in your team's goal. Humanize the goal. Put a face and a name to it. Paint a picture of what the outcome will feel like when the team achieves it. Then ask team members how they would feel if their team fails; ask them to get in touch with those feelings too. By continually reminding people of the meaning and consequences of their work, you reinforce their dedication to the goal.

ASSUME

Here is where many leaders make their first mistake. They assume that their teammates are not (pick one) good enough, skilled enough, focused enough, committed enough, or tenacious enough. Some leaders sabotage their chances for success right from the start by not giving their team members the benefit of the doubt—by presuming that they can't function creatively without the leader's constant oversight. There's a fine line between productively monitoring and encouraging the team and counterproductively micromanaging it. If you can't assume that your team's intentions and skills are good, you may end up creating a self-fulfilling prophecy of doom. The more your actions communicate that you don't believe in them, the more your team will doubt its own skills and progress. It may feel unnatural and uncomfortable, but you must give your people the confidence and the freedom to tackle the task at hand. If you follow the steps in chapter 3, "Connect," these feelings will be mitigated, because you will have connected with your team and built an initial level of trust. Giving your people the room to start the process of achieving the goal begins a very important next phase in building a deeper level of trust with them—and this can happen only by taking a step back, allowing them to choose their own ways to tackle the problem.

ASSESS

Leaders may fall into another trap during the periodic assessment of team progress. Here let me emphasize the word *team*, because that's the appropriate unit of analysis when assessing your teammates' work. By focusing on *team* progress, you're separating the whole output from the individual contributions, as if it were in the center of a lazy Susan, rotating so all participants may look at it impartially from all angles. If the assessment is focused solely on individual contributions and progress, you may be inspiring fear and distrust, which shuts down creativity, candor, and true progress—exactly the things you're trying to assess in the first place.

ASSURE

When teams take on OTH goals, they need to be reminded that it's OK for things to be hard, that it's OK to be uncertain and afraid, and that if you're failing, it's OK to ask for help. You press on anyway. Assuring and reassuring your team is a never-ending process. Your job as the team leader is to hear your team's doubts and concerns but then help them reframe these challenges in a positive manner. The team leader must be able to provide continual assurance that the team's efforts matter and contribute to achievement. From the janitor to the junior manager to the jack-of-all-trades superstar, all team members must become convinced that their work matters and that the team is counting on them.

APPRECIATE

Like the other components of the A in the CARE loop, showing your appreciation isn't so much a distinct phase as it is a consistent action. Think of the actions of appreciation and assurance as swim buddies—they go hand in hand. When you're assuring someone that the job they're doing is important or that they can do it, don't forget to tell them you appreciate the effort they've made so far. How you say it, when you say it, and what specifically you are calling out will ensure that your acts of appreciation are long-lasting and impactful. For instance, when I was leading my company, I borrowed yet another tradition from my time with the SEALs. We installed a large brass bell that anyone could ring to announce an accomplishment or to show appreciation for someone's contributions toward reaching a goal. You rang the bell just once unless you were moving to a new team (leaving the company); then you rang it three times, just as in SEAL training. Don't be afraid to create your own rituals or to borrow this one to make the act of appreciation an integral part of your team's culture.

Remember, this book is about building unstoppable teams. These kinds of teams aren't assembled to accomplish easily attainable goals, such as so-called SMART goals—

specific, measurable, achievable, relevant, and time-bound. I'm talking about transformative objectives that require the best from everyone, not just contributions from a few outstanding individuals. SMART goal setting works just fine when the course of action is clear and the goal is fully understood, but when you're working outside the known and achievable, unstoppable teams, bolstered by the five As of Achievement, are required.

Extreme examples of OTH goals are building the Panama Canal, the Manhattan Project, and President Kennedy's promise to "put a man on the moon within ten years." It's easy to state a bold vision, but until a leader creates a reason to believe, lofty visions remain nothing more than dreams. OTH goals are not achieved overnight. They can require years of relentless action while dealing with failures, setbacks, and the toughest enemy: doubt. A team leader's first responsibility is keeping the team connected to the purpose while reminding them of the reasons they can achieve their goal.

A little over sixty years ago, the Russians put *Sputnik 1* into orbit. Mankind's first satellite launched two nations on a race to explore space. Three years later, John Kennedy narrowly defeated Richard Nixon to become the youngest president in US history. The nation was divided after decades of bloodshed, from World War I to the Korean War. President Kennedy recognized that a common goal could rally the country; he sought an OTH goal that the country could aspire to achieve.

While delivering a speech to Congress on May 25, 1961, four months after taking office, he challenged the nation to "put a man on the moon by the end of the decade." At a time when America was still trying to understand how to launch a satellite, the idea of putting a man on the moon in less than ten years was the definition of an OTH goal. There was no clearly identifiable way to accomplish it. Not only were there competing approaches, but there were also a series of challenging tasks that would need to be accomplished before someone could even take a step toward the moon. This lofty lunar vision required a team of teams to tackle a series of OTH goals, such as:

- Creating a worldwide satellite communication infrastructure for both audible and visual communications. Besides the need to communicate with the astronauts, it wouldn't do the American people any good if they couldn't hear or see an American land and walk on the moon!
- Building a separate satellite system for worldwide weather observations to know when and where to launch and recover spacecraft.
- Designing, testing, and refining rocket boosters and fuels capable of launching manned spacecraft.

- Inventing a lunar spacecraft.
- Executing preparatory unmanned space explorations.

Each one of these goals, and there were many more, was an OTH. As President Kennedy rightfully saw it, putting a man on the moon would involve the efforts of every single American:

> I believe that this nation should commit itself to achieving the goal, before this decade is out, of landing a man on the moon and returning him safely to the earth. . . . But in a very real sense, it will not be one man going to the moon—if we make this judgment affirmatively, it will be an entire nation. For all of us must work to put him there.

As NASA leaders quickly realized, their OTH goal would depend on best guesses, trial-and-error efforts, and numerous course corrections over the next decade. As they dug in, NASA teams often would learn something new or develop a new technology that would change their minds and hence their course of action on how to accomplish the goal. That's how unstoppable teams work. They swarm a problem from multiple angles before they single out one approach. They realize that when you're venturing into unknown waters, it's all hands on deck. This process of swarming for solutions, as opposed to sending off individuals to work in silos, is the essence of what unstoppable teams do. They don't rely on one person for the solution; everyone pitches in without regard for individual glory. But this selfless attitude does not happen magically; that's why the CARE loop is so important.

President Kennedy knew that his OTH goal would require an unconventional approach and an extraordinary leader to provide the action plan and set the tone for the day-to-day work. He put the project under the leadership of James E. Webb, a business executive and bureaucrat who understood the inner workings of Washington and defense contractors. Webb was not a scientist and knew next to nothing about space and rocketry. However, he did know how to build teams that could achieve the seemingly impossible. During his time leading NASA, from 1961 to 1968, its ranks swelled to thirty-five thousand employees and over four hundred thousand contractors. Webb assumed that he would get the best from NASA's scientists, but he also engaged universities throughout America to contribute to the effort.

Webb used Kennedy's aspirational message to unify a team of unstoppables at all levels of the organization. As a popular anecdote has it, the president toured the newly formed NASA space center in 1962. He stopped to chat with a janitor who was mopping the floor and said, "Hi, I'm Jack Kennedy. What are you doing?" to which the janitor responded, "Well, Mr. President, I'm helping put a man on the moon."

The more vivid and inclusive you can make your call to action, the deeper the connection will be to the hearts and minds of your teammates. Every mission starts with identifying the meaning behind the mission, so as to give people something to aspire to achieve. Some aspirations, such as hunting war criminals, are more obviously worthwhile than others.

Even so, there will be many times at work or in your community when you'll need to confront an OTH goal. Undoubtedly you will all sometimes feel afraid when you do. People grapple with fear differently, but the more you can connect your teammates with the reasons for their commitment, the more fuel they will have to fight back those personal fears and keep forging ahead.

Fear fills the void when we're confronted by the unknown. The five A's of Achievement will help you manage your own fears, too. Unstoppable teams come to believe that even fear of the unknown is something they can take on together. By creating aspirational goals, by assuming the best of your team, by assessing team progress without making the mistakes and interim failures personal, by assuring the team that they can take on unheard-of tasks, and finally by appreciating their commitment and progress, you make an environment for your teammates to perform at the highest levels. This approach to achievement creates the habits and rituals that can bring a murky horizon into better focus and make otherwise unimaginable goals possible.

I had many opportunities to test these ideas as a SEAL, but I also learned about the value of the five A's when I was building my fitness-equipment business. For more than eight years, I managed our company's relationship with Walmart, our biggest retailer. Walmart challenged us to produce great products at lower prices, so its customers could live better lives—the company's tagline.

To understand the OTH challenges we faced in working with Walmart, let me give you some context. Many companies make a living selling their products directly to consumers on television (and the Internet), as part of the direct-response (DR) industry. DR is a high risk/high reward business that has grown into a multibillion-dollar sector with industry verticals built around each node of the supply chain, from manufacturing to call centers to media buying to e-commerce and more. Most DR companies are pluralistic when it comes to the types of products they sell, and it's a good risk-sharing strategy to sell different products in multiple categories. A company might sell home products (mops and window cleaners), beauty products (skin-care items and wrinkle removers), and fitness products. It's a well-developed strategy, and most retailers have established their own departments for selling these products. The "As Seen on TV" (ASOTV) re-

tail department has its own buyer responsible for oversee-
ing its highly valuable in-store shelf space, typically at the
front of the store. Though we used a DR approach to launching Perfect Pushup, we did not (and do not) consider our
product line an ASOTV brand.

Our Perfect Pushup infomercial quickly gained trac-
tion as one of the leading infomercials in the country, and
that got us noticed by Walmart's ASOTV buyer. At the time,
we were an extremely small company, with five employees
and less than a million dollars in sales. We used external
sales representatives to help us get into the leading retail
stores. We had successfully launched retail programs with
Dick's, Sports Authority, Big 5, and a handful of other sporting goods retailers. We were busy and hadn't really thought
about selling in Walmart until we received a call from our
lead sales rep, Ray, who said, "I've got good news and really
bad news. What do you want to hear first?"

I went for the latter.

"Walmart is going to take a product competitive to yours
that is half the price of what you're selling on TV." He waited
a moment for me to take in that bad news before adding,
"That means you've lost mass retail, which then means
you're going to have to cut your price to even stay on the
shelves of your current retailers." We had just started our
TV ad campaign less than six months before, and already
a savvy competitor was going head-to-head with us, with

a similar name, no less, and a product that was 50 percent cheaper than ours. I chewed on his comments for a few moments before asking him, "And the good news is?"

He chuckled and continued. "Walmart likes your brand better, and they'll buy yours if you build them one that's half the price of your current one." He laughed again and added the kicker: "Oh, yeah, and it needs to be delivered in ninety days to forty-four distribution centers."

The original Perfect Pushup took ninety days to be designed by top California designer Steven G. Hauser, one of only fifty fellows of the Industrial Designers Society of America. The design was completed only after we knew exactly what the specifications were. Our products were built in China, and just carving the steel molds for the plastic parts could take up to forty-five days after testing. Then there was the time needed to build the products, followed by time needed to ship them across the Pacific Ocean—not to mention getting them through US customs and on trucks to be delivered to forty-four Walmart warehouses. The best-case scenario was six months—if you knew exactly what you were building and your manufacturer had a production line available to dedicate to your new product. Of course, Ray knew all of this, which is why he had laughed when he was delivering the supposedly good news. He felt he already knew the outcome: not possible.

But then . . . we didn't laugh back. Instead, I asked him,

"How much time do we have to tell Walmart of our intentions?" That caught Ray by surprise.

"Alden, you can't be serious—there's no way you can build something that fast. Not even the big guys can do it that quickly. You don't have the supply-chain horsepower to get it done. Walmart's not going to happen."

But I persisted. "Ray, how much time do we have?"

"Twenty-four hours," he said flatly.

The minute I hung up the phone, my small team went into overdrive. Mark, my cofounder and head of operations, called our manufacturer to see if he would give us a production line and expedite tooling; Andrew, the CFO, called the bank to start the process for an extension on our line of credit. I called our designer, who had already told us he was retired after the Perfect Pushup. We needed each of these three parties to sign on if we had a shot at reaching this OTH goal. As with every unstoppable team, we needed a bond with our external partners that was every bit as strong as the one we'd formed internally. Fortunately, each of these partners signed on to our aspiration, from our Chinese manufacturer to our banker to our semiretired designer, who couldn't help grumbling, "You'd better get to my office tomorrow; we've got work to do."

In less than sixty days after Ray's phone call, we went into production of our new design; on the ninetieth day, the Perfect Pushup Basic was featured on the shelves of Walmart stores, and within six months we had sold more than one million units of our "ninety-day wonder" to Walmart alone. Pulling off this OTH goal required all kinds of feats of unstoppability, not least of which was our team's commitment to the CARE loop.

This achievement occurred under extreme conditions, with no lines of sight into the dangerous waters beyond the horizon, but we'd already built a strong foundation of trust, commitment, and love for each other. We shared the same aspirations. That made it possible for us to block out the noise and confront our fears and self-doubts without getting stuck, to learn fast without doing more harm than good. The risk of doing more harm than good becomes even greater when you're taking on OTH goals, whether you're chasing terrorists, launching must-not-fail products, or treating children facing life-threatening illnesses.

The Latin maxim *Primum non nocere,* "First, do no harm," expresses an idea suggested in the Hippocratic oath, reminding medical professionals to take their unique responsibility and power seriously by holding themselves accountable for the potential consequences of their actions. Today the phrase is considered to refer to preventable harm, which is the fourteenth leading cause of morbidity and mortality in hospitals around the world. Incorrect diagnosis, improper medication, administrative errors, and on-site infections are just a few of the reasons preventable harm remains a top killer. Tackling preventable harm is challenging because of the complexity of safe health care. It's seldom just one doctor, one procedure, or one department that determines the outcome. For example, administrative errors account for up to half of all medical errors in primary care, while hospital infections affect fourteen of every hundred patients. The costs associated with preventable harm are staggering. An estimated 15 percent of all health spending around the world goes to treating it. In the United States, medication errors alone cost over $40 billion annually. The irony of preventable harm is that most medical professionals know how to avoid it in a single case; the problem arises when you try to scale the solution across multiple diverse departments within a hospital. As administrators of Boston Children's Hospital (BCH) found out, the cure for preventable harm comes from everyone teaming up to prevent it.

By any measure, BCH's success has been astonishing. In *US News & World Report* rankings, BCH has been in the top ten for eighteen years in a row; for five years, it has held the number-one spot. What's the staff's magic? How do they consistently find ways to be the best—to be an unstoppable team? I visited them to learn about their mission and their aspiration to reduce preventable harm to zero. It's a remarkable OTH that requires every person, from doorman to doctor, to be involved. Here's a recap of their approach:

- All hands on deck, all the time. They don't use these exact words, but that's their focus—to hold every person, every employee, responsible and accountable for reaching the goal.
- High Reliability Training, wherein trust, reporting, and continuous improvement are required.
- Self-reporting of mistakes.
- Daily safety briefings with participation from personnel in all departments.
- Error-prevention training for more than fourteen thousand employees and leaders.

These actions support BCH's goals, but perhaps the most critical action is its focus on expanding the definition of preventable harm, not just to patients but also to staff. By including and tracking the reduction of preventable harm to its workers, BCH fosters a caring environment for both those receiving the care and those giving it. By including the safety of their staff in the OTH of achieving zero preventable harm, all members become more willing participants in reducing the role that human ego plays in the process. By creating a culture in which employees are encouraged to report mistakes, to learn and improve, BCH ensures that its employees' good intentions are aligned with practices that reduce preventable harm. In many organizations, it's not natural to self-report your mistakes, much less encouraged, yet that is one of the tenets that has made BCH unstoppable. Employees are encouraged and even rewarded for acknowledging their mistakes; they receive regular training and professional development to make mistakes even rarer. In this way, BCH shows that it cares for its employees just as much as it cares for its patients. When you conduct all-hands meetings five days a week and spend millions more training every single person on your staff on harm prevention, you are both connecting with individuals and giving them the tools to achieve a visionary goal. BCH hasn't yet eliminated preventable harm completely, but it has dramatically reduced it.

As the BCH story shows, achievement is rarely contained within any one team, department, or company. In addition, fear of the unknown is a reality for every team with high aspirations. It's not something to be avoided. Indeed, the best leaders turn fear on its head by helping their teams find personal meaning in the goal, by assuming that the team has what it takes to succeed (and providing what's missing if necessary), by providing constructive feedback and assessments as the team makes progress (or goes off track), and by showing all members that they are valued and appreciated for their contributions. As you do this, you will begin to cultivate the next element that unstoppable teams need: respect.

C.A.R.E. Loop

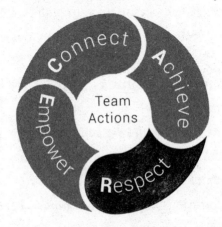

CHAPTER 5

RESPECT

"Lew-ten-ant Mills, this here camera is worth more than what the government pays ya in a year, so don't drop it, ya hear me?" Colonel Stones (not his actual name) wasn't joking. He opened a black case, pulled out what looked like a regular 35mm film-loaded camera, pointed it at me, and said, "Say cheeeese." I played along, giving him a halfhearted smile while he snapped the photo. Next, he turned the camera around to face me and pushed a button revealing my photo on a small LCD screen. I leaned in closer and looked incredulously at the photo that had seemed to appear magically on the screen. He registered the look of surprise on my face: "This here is a first-generation digital camera, and it's what the team I select is gonna use on this next mission." I was still processing his last comment, as he continued: "The general wants to see the whites of the son-of-a-bitch's eyes before we grab him. Whatever team puts the best plan together gets to sign for this here $34,000 camera and go on a camping trip." That "camping trip" would take us into the mountains of Bosnia to hunt a war criminal called Doctor Death.

When I was deployed to Bosnia in 1997, team leaders competed against other special-forces units for assignments, in this case to go after Doctor Death. The senior Army officer in charge was Colonel Stones, to whom I reported in Sarajevo, Bosnia-Herzegovina. On several occasions, he had openly voiced his concerns about a "waterborne" unit, like the SEALs, competing for "land-based" missions. Colonel Stones had spent his career working in Army Special Operations as both a Ranger and a Green Beret. His preconceived notion was that SEALs belonged in the water, and Army units belonged on land. This pro-Army attitude was a long-standing challenge for all SEAL platoon commanders. We were constantly having to justify our land-based skills to our Army counterparts, a situation that always came with an added challenge because our Army brethren were often our operational bosses too. Navy SEALs, Green Berets, Army Rangers, Delta Force, and many other special-forces units report to Special Operations Command, which for the longest time was run by Army generals. I bring up this point because it's not surprising that Army soldiers like to work with Army soldiers. There's a comfort level in working with people who have been through the same training and consequently think and act in a similar fashion. The same holds true in the corporate world. People find comfort in working with people who have been trained to think and act like them.

But good ol' Colonel Stones was no normal Army officer; he was open to competing perspectives. It helped that he had closely observed my platoon and my leadership style while stationed in Sarajevo. Every morning he ran a daily briefing that included military professionals from the United States and Europe. Colonel Stones oversaw special-operations missions in Bosnia for Operation Joint Guard, and he dealt with a wide array of personalities and military mind-sets among the French, German, and Dutch, as well as his American assets of Army, Air Force, Marines, and one Navy SEAL platoon—Hotel Platoon, my team. At the end of each briefing, he gave attendees from each of the groups the opportunity to make an announcement. I made the same announcement every day. I offered anyone in the room or their direct reports an opportunity to join our platoon's daily workout sessions. At first people scoffed at my announcement: "Why would I ever want to go through a workout with Navy SEALs?" So I softened my approach to be more inclusive and eventually convinced a few administrative staff to join our daily workouts. My platoon mates turned into quasi–personal trainers, helping others do pullups and pushups. My Sarajevo team-building approach wasn't some sophisticated ten-point strategy for building better culture; it was a simple idea to get more people in the unit to exercise together. Our mantra in SEAL Team is "the platoon that works out together stays together." We simply extended that mantra to Colonel Stones's unit.

Here we were, in the middle of a war zone, trying to keep a shaky peace accord in place, and for a portion of every day we helped others get in shape. My SEAL platoon, a squad of eight SEALs, was relegated to sleeping in a converted twenty-foot shipping container. (Ah, the smells—nothing quite like it!) There were sniper tarps thirty feet high surrounding the perimeter of our compound and numerous minefields just outside the gates. Our workout area was limited to a makeshift pullup bar, a few wooden boxes, and a circular dirt track in front of headquarters. As our attendance grew, so did the colonel's respect for our willingness to work with all the different units of his command, while building camaraderie along the way. When it came time to select a unit to hunt Doctor Death, Colonel Stones invited us to prepare a pitch for the mission.

The colonel gave my platoon forty-eight hours to experiment with the digital camera, along with the other equipment required to download and send digital files from deep in the mountains. As you might imagine, a first-generation digital camera (this was 1997) recorded about a two-megabyte picture that downloaded via cable to a laptop computer (in this case a Toshiba Portégé). None of the electronic gear was "ruggedized," meaning it wasn't waterproof, shockproof, or dirtproof, and each piece required its own unique batteries. Protecting the equipment was one thing; making sure we had enough batteries was quite another challenge. There wasn't a Best Buy in Sarajevo or an Amazon distribution center or even a FedEx delivery outpost. We figured we needed about forty Portégé laptop batteries to complete the mission. We had two. Within a couple hours of tinkering with the equipment, we realized that the challenge of this mission would be figuring out a way to power these electronics. Our squad split into teams of two to brainstorm ideas on how to overcome this obstacle. One teammate, nicknamed Sully, asked for permission to essentially destroy a piece of electronic measuring equipment called a multimeter. Though we didn't have thirty-eight Toshiba batteries, we did have a plentiful supply of US military standard radio batteries called 5590s. These batteries powered practically every single variant of military radio, and the command had hundreds of them. While we sat on bunks inside our "container condo" discussing various ideas, Sully quietly waited until we finished before unveiling his idea. He had cannibalized wires from the multimeter, rewired them to the laptop's battery leads, and made male fittings that could mate with the female connectors of the standard-issue military batteries. Best of all, his Frankenstein system worked!

We spent the next twenty-four hours planning every aspect of the mission, from how to get to and from our observation location to operating the surveillance system to brainstorming all the things that could go wrong (and creating contingencies for each one). When we presented our plan to Colonel Stones a day later, his first question wasn't about where we would position ourselves. He cut right to the heart of the matter: "How'd you boys solve the battery problem?" I gave him a high-level short answer, and then Sully demonstrated his innovation. Stones smiled, asked for our mission briefing, and then grilled us for about an hour on the different elements of the plan before granting the mission to us. As we were departing, I asked him how the other team solved the battery problem. He grimaced and said, "They called their unit back in North Carolina and was having fellas buy up all the batteries they could find and then they were going to fly 'em over here on one of the weekly replenishment flights."

We hadn't even executed the mission yet, but we had

already demonstrated our team dynamics to the colonel. Each teammate's opinion was respected in the planning process. We were all in it together, and hearing everyone's concerns and points of view had helped sharpen our mission planning. It not only made our plan better, but also made everyone an owner of the mission. Everyone had played a role in the plan; even those who wouldn't be going on the mission were actively involved in all elements of the planning. (We planned to rotate a couple of teammates onto the mission, depending on how long it took to find Doctor Death.) Many of us "donated" our own gear to help ruggedize the electronic equipment, which meant cutting up wetsuits and drybags to create protective layers for the camera and the laptop. We were all in.

Fast-forward ten years and replace Colonel Stones with the Walmart buyer, the competing special-operations teams with competitive companies producing similar products, and SEAL swim buddies with Perfect Fitness employees. You will find lots of similarities. Sure, the worst-case scenarios aren't the same—nobody was going to get injured or killed if we didn't land the Walmart deal—but both outcomes were fraught with unknown risks, and success depended on the actions of many. In much the same way that Colonel Stones decided to grant us an opportunity to present our mission, the Walmart buyer (from the story in

chapter 4) granted the Perfect Pushup team a chance to produce a different version of our product at a lower price. We
gained Colonel Stones's respect by the way we treated his
unit's personnel, and the Walmart buyer respected the fact
that we were first to market and that we understood that he
needed a lower-cost product for his division to be successful. With both teams, we realized that the situation required
us to reset our expectations and to abandon our preconcep-
tions to help achieve larger goals. Would it have been easier
and faster if our SEAL platoon had worked out alone instead
of inviting people, many of whom were quite out of shape,
to join us? Absolutely. Our workouts took twice as long, and
many teammates ended up doing a second workout later
in the day. And with Walmart, too, our team debated long
and hard the merits of essentially "knocking off" our first-
generation product to create something specifically for the
mega-retailer. The seemingly impossible deadline, the risks
of rapid design, and low-margin sales were just a few of the
elements that made this decision difficult. However, we respected Walmart for the customer base it represented, those
who might not be able to afford a $40 pushup device but who
still sought quality fitness products. It was a pivotal decision
for our little company, a "bet it all" decision that required us
to go all in to make that product work. Once we decided to
move forward, we committed ourselves to doing whatever
it would take to become a long-term Walmart partner; to

accomplish this we had to earn the trust and respect of the buyer.

As you will see with other examples of team dynamics, such as caring for customers or communities, the way the team operates in public is a direct reflection of how they treat each other in private. If you want your team to care about their customers, show them how to care for each other. This sets the example that carries forward in all interactions. It sounds obvious, right? Still, I can't tell you how many times I've run into leaders who think they can fake it, turning on the charm and sincerity only when it matters. As a team leader, you reap what you sow. Your team will act the way you do.

Respect—from within the team and for the team—must be earned. Earning it is the right thing to do for its own sake, but it also has a deep impact on a team's performance and its ability to gain visibility and resources from others. *Respect* as a verb is not a passive trait; it's all the actions you take within your team and outside the team to shine a light on the team's skills and capabilities and to show how the team can contribute to others' success. Your job as a team builder is to take the lead highlighting other people's skills and articulating how those capabilities can help the team. Remember, people are inherently selfish. We think inward before thinking outward. Your deference to a person's ability broadcasts that person's strengths to teammates who might not be aware of them. When you take this action of acknowledgment, people tend to reciprocate by opening their eyes and minds to seeing the strengths in others.

Mutual respect is a powerful adhesive when the team comes under pressure. People who feel respected are more confident to express their ideas. They aren't wasting energy thinking of how not to look stupid; instead they focus on using their abilities to help the team solve the problem. Put simply, respect fuels greater levels of contribution. When you create an environment of mutual respect, you also eliminate the fear of being ignored, humiliated, or victimized. As we saw in the previous chapter, removing ego and fear from the equation also makes it possible for teammates to acknowledge their mistakes and to take the necessary steps to learn and grow.

WHAT COMES AROUND GOES AROUND

Three elements of respect are what I call the three Rs: Realize, Recognize, and Require. These actions establish an environment of respect that, when interwoven with the trust you have built and the direction you have set forth, will create a platform for developing empowered teammates. Here's how I define the three Rs of Respect:

1. **REALIZE.** Respect comes from two places: from your authority and from your actions; the respect gar-

nered from the latter is more valuable and more sustainable than the former.

2. **RECOGNIZE.** Respect derives from results. As a team builder, it's your job to bring forth and acknowledge the superpowers of each of your teammates.

3. **REQUIRE.** Respect isn't a nice-to-have; it's a requirement, and it needs to be shared and reciprocated.

Besides setting and communicating the team's direction and progress, your primary role as team leader is to spot the skills and abilities that will ensure team success. You can have a wonderfully trusting team, but if they don't have the skills and abilities required to accomplish the task at hand, success will be very difficult to find. From recruitment to retainment, respecting people's contributions to the team is essential to team unity. Your position of power gives you a head start, but if your actions don't support an environment of respect, you can't hope to create an unstoppable team. Unfortunately, many leaders hide behind their authority and use it as an excuse not to follow up on their promises. Worse, some are so insecure or proud that they feel threatened by people with better skills and find reasons to move top people out of the team. The result? A group of individuals surrounding a weak and insecure leader who uses his position to demand one-way respect. This dynamic often plays out in failing companies and troubled countries; fear is a poor, even dangerous, substitute for leadership.

When leaders openly acknowledge the contributions of others, guess what happens? Teammates want to contribute *more*. As much as humans can be selfish, it's also in our nature to want to contribute to a cause, something larger than our individual goals and self-interests. The best team members come to realize that they are never as strong alone as they are when they are surrounded by others who bring diverse perspectives and different levels of experience to the team. The team comes to recognize its interdependency and thrives on mutual respect to get things done. I have experienced this shared sense of purpose in SEAL Team, but I have also experienced it leading a community action group to pass a $30 million school bond.

THE THREE Rs IN ACTION

One Sunday afternoon in late August 2014, my wife and I found ourselves alone while our four boys were playing with friends down the street. We don't get these moments very often, and when we do, we do very boring things, like read the newspaper or watch a sporting event on TV. This time the newspapers had won our attention. We had just started diving into the Sunday papers when our doorbell rang. It was odd to hear it because most of the time our kids or their friends just barge right through the front door without so much as a knock or even a greeting. (If we get a greeting, it's usually "I'm hungry! When's dinner?")

Our surprise guest was Ashley, one of our elected school board members, who greeted me with a gentle smile. "Hiya, Alden. Just who I'm looking for. Do you have a few minutes?" Ashley is a friend and a multiyear board member whom we respect for her years of service to our community and to the local public schools. In our neighborhood, the schools are the town's lifeblood. Parents and community groups raise money every year to support physical education, art, music, shop, and computer labs, all of which aren't funded by the state, as they once were. Now they're community-funded school programs. My wife and I joined the community campaign to raise these funds shortly after our first child started kindergarten. We had come to know Ashley through these annual efforts as we worked closely with the school board members. When Ashley arrived at our door, my wife and I had just stepped down after two years leading the communal campaign to raise over $1 million annually to fund these essential classes.

Ashley wasn't a routine visitor to our house, so I knew something was up. The Sunday papers could wait. After a few pleasantries, she disclosed the purpose of her visit. For a variety of very good reasons, the school board had decided that now was the time to address our overpopulated schools. The building that housed kindergarten through fifth grade had been built for 440 kids, but current enrollment was over 800. The middle school, sixth through eighth grades, was a little less overcrowded, thanks to mobile classrooms that we were renting. The school board had decided to issue a $30 million bond to expand the school buildings. That made good sense, but the board decided to get the town to vote on the bond within ninety days—an OTH goal. That was a very tight schedule, which made it even more challenging because we needed a supermajority of 67 percent for the bond measure to pass, because this was an off year for elections.

As Ashley explained the details, my mind was already racing to understand how to make this happen. I didn't get very far in my thinking, because I had never run a community bond campaign. I was still daydreaming when she put the question to me: "Alden, will you run the campaign?" I looked at my wife, who put her hands up and said, "Don't look at me. She's asking you!"

I said, "Ashley, I have *no* clue what's involved or how to run a bond campaign."

She smiled and said, "We know, but not to worry. There are consultants you can hire."

Her response raised another obvious question for me. "And where am I going to get the money to hire these consultants?"

Her answer came quickly: "With the money your team is going to raise to advertise the bond measure."

Now my mind was really sprinting, and I thought aloud. "So let me get this straight. You want to put a team together to raise money to raise awareness so as to convince 67 percent of our community to vote in favor of raising their taxes?"

Ashley nodded. "And you have a little less than ninety days to do it. . . . So whaddya say? Are you in?"

How could I say no?

The next ninety days were a blur, and in hindsight I'm glad I told my Perfect Fitness team what I was doing, because little did I know I had just accepted a full-time volunteer job. No sooner had Ashley left the house than I started writing down the names of the dream team I'd be asking to join me on this mission. Key positions needed to be filled, and not just people who had the right capabilities; they had to be willing to contribute countless hours of their time for free. Oh, and we needed to raise roughly $35,000 (not tax deductible, I might add!) in two weeks to fund the campaign. I needed a chief financial officer, a chief fund-raiser and sales leader, and a public relations officer. And then there was the CAO—the chief awareness officer—the most time-consuming role, to get the word out. Ashley didn't know it at the time, but my wife and I had been invited to dinner that very evening at the home of the couple who had just relieved us as leaders of the annual community fundraising committee. I figured there was no time like the present to start recruiting. I asked the dinner party guests a question: "Who here would like to improve our schools?"

I spent twenty minutes recapping my conversation with Ashley and finished with an open-ended question: "Who's in?" Thankfully, this group of ten friends were well-known volunteers in the community, and even though they were perpetually busy as parents, executives, and part-time volunteers for everything from coaching to coordinating school lunches, they all raised their hands. That evening was day one of ninety days of flat-out campaign work. Bank accounts, ballot registration, fundraising, door-to-door marketing awareness teams, signs, bumper stickers, community outreach meetings, architecture concept drawings, newspaper interviews, social media commentary, and phone-athons—they all became part of our plan. We developed a simple slogan, "Yes on Measure D." Within a few days, we had enlisted close to a hundred volunteers to get the message out to our community.

Taking a page from my training as a Navy SEAL, the campaign team resembled a team of teams, from the fundraising team to the marketing awareness teams. Each team had a team leader—more of a player/coach than a manager. Team leaders didn't tell people what to do; they did the same work as the rest but also offered guidance and a big-picture view of our progress. Every person needed to post signs, knock on doors, host info-receptions, and participate in phone-athons. The superintendent of schools was part of the team, right along with parents, principals, and board members. This setup worked well because everyone's efforts were respected and essential. Some volunteers could work only evenings; others, only weekends; but they all knew their efforts were making a difference and were appreciated. We would hold informal gatherings at my home to give updates (along with weekly electronic updates tracking progress and highlighting things to do). My first and last comments always focused on acknowledging and appreciating everyone's efforts. The only way this campaign was going to succeed was through mass participation focused on one goal: getting more than 67 percent of the vote in our favor. It was a guerrilla effort. Our plan was constantly updated and improved as people came up with new and better ideas. Of course, new ideas are only as good as those who are willing to own them. This simple process of listening and learning from others created mutual respect among the volunteers—so much so that we ended up calling ourselves the Bond Team (pun intended). We even gave ourselves and each other nicknames derived from James Bond films. We needed some levity to keep the work fun, especially when we had to handle some of the team's least favorite tasks, such as cold-calling. It was, to say the least, a real "bonding" experience.

I am certain we made all kinds of mistakes, but they weren't what we focused on. Our focus was on getting as many people as possible to participate to help pass the bond measure. We didn't worry about mistakes; we shared them, so they wouldn't be repeated, and we kept our focus on taking daily action toward our objective.

Our process worked. Exactly ninety days from the time Ashley asked for our help, the Bond Team's efforts paid off, with over 72 percent voting in favor of Measure D. Our process was messy, we had incomplete information, the landscape was constantly changing, our team was rotating people, and at any given time I couldn't tell you exactly what everyone was doing. It was an OTH operation all the way. But unstoppable teams are built for just those kinds of situations. That's why, as a leader, it's so important for you to build a strong leadership platform for yourself, and then to implement the CARE loop when you recruit your team. As the leader of this wild group of volunteers, I tried not to miss an opportunity to highlight the actions of others. We succeeded because of the Bond Team's efforts. All I did was create the foundation for their actions. I served them, they served the community, and in turn the community responded by passing the bond measure.

The bond campaign is a great example of team building in crisis to tackle OTH goals. Leading a team of volunteers may be the hardest task any leader will face. Teams perform in three basic areas: crisis, creativity, and productivity. All teams must be able to perform well in all three elements. Our Bond Team was essentially created in crisis (ninety days to achieve an objective). We used creativity to maximize our efforts, and we tracked our productivity by polling to gauge our effectiveness. There were no bonuses, promotions, or stock shares at stake; the only equity to be earned was in being a part of something for our kids and the community's future. On any given day, our "workers" could choose to stop working. Our team was 99 percent volunteers (we hired one consultant), and the success of our campaign was completely dependent on everyone's willingness to donate time and effort.

Here's a question for you: Do you think leading a team of volunteers is different from leading a team of employees (who get paid to work) or a team of Navy SEALs? Before you answer, think about how you would treat volunteers—people who have decided to give up free time to work with you toward a common goal. If they make a mistake, do you treat them differently than paid employees or platoon mates? Do you motivate them differently? How do you speak to volunteers? Are you appreciative of their time and commitment, or do you expect them to carry out your commands? Who works for whom when everyone is a volunteer? In a sense, every team is made up of volunteers, whether they're getting paid a salary or not. Paid employees may show up for your meeting, but if you want them to sign on to your mission, to "own it," then you need to treat every team member the same way. Obviously, there are differences in workload and expectations, depending on the circumstances, but the approach should be the same. That's because *we are all volunteers*. Whether the people you interact with are SEALs or software engineers, they all have some choice as to where they decide to work, how much effort and commitment they're willing to make, and how deeply engaged in the effort they'll be. Think back to the Gallup survey I mentioned in chapter 3. Are your teammates engaged? Or are they simply present? Are they unstoppable or just available?

You might think that the best salaries and perks attract the best people and get the most out of them, but conventional rewards, while necessary, almost never produce the level of commitment and mutual respect I'm talking about. If you want to motivate people, you must set the right tone, from how to speak to them to what you do for them. They watch your every move. Respect demands trust and vice versa; one begets the other. Trust provides a safety net, and respect is the fuel that energizes the team in tough times. According to Professor Christine Porath of Georgetown

University, who conducted a global study research project (with *Harvard Business Review* and Tony Schwartz, CEO of the Energy Project) involving more than twenty thousand people, "When it comes to garnering commitment and engagement from employees, there is one thing that leaders need to demonstrate: Respect."[1]

Shockingly, this research found that more than half (54 percent) of the participants reported they don't receive regular respect from their leaders. The study showed a direct link between respect and engagement. Not only were high-respect environments correlated with high engagement, but Porath and her teammates also discovered a host of positive correlations of respect to performance:

Those that get respect from their leaders reported 56% better health and well-being, 1.72 times more trust and safety, 89% greater enjoyment and satisfaction with their jobs, 92% greater focus and prioritization, and 1.26 times more meaning and significance. Those that feel respected by their leaders were also 1.1 times more likely to stay with their organizations than those that didn't.[2]

When Doug Conant became CEO of Campbell Soup in 2001, he viewed respect as a cornerstone of his turnaround strategy. The company had lost over half its market value, conducted a large round of layoffs, and faced declining revenues. A Gallup researcher reported that the company's engagement statistics "were the worst for any Fortune 500 firm ever polled."[3] Conant spent the next nine years never missing the opportunity to show respect for the contributions of the twenty thousand people of Campbell Soup. Conant and his leadership team developed the Campbell Promise: "Campbell valuing people. People valuing Campbell."[4] He intentionally led with the importance of Campbell valuing people; he wanted people to know they are valued and respected. He reinforced the promise with a ten-point pledge as to how he intended to lead, and his first point was: "We will treat you with respect and dignity." He personally sent more than thirty thousand thank-you notes to show his respect for employees' efforts. His actions set the tone for his 350 senior leaders to emulate, and they did. By 2010 the company was setting all-time performance records while outpacing the S&P 500 fivefold.

Respect is earned by your contribution to the team's success, and sometimes it's possible to make a meaningful contribution only when you remove the blinders of ego. All too often, team builders mistakenly presume that the best ideas will come only from the most experienced team members. It happens even in the military: "New meat" or "FNGs" (fucking new guys) are what we would call SEALs on their first deployment, and we had one on our mission to hunt

Doctor Death. His nickname was Cappy and he earned a spot on the first wave of the mission because he was a medic. He lacked experience in the field, but he more than made up for that by working hard and listening more than he talked. About two days into the hunt, we received word from Colonel Stones that he was about to abort the mission because the pictures we were sending back were too blurry; the digital camera's autofocus couldn't keep up with speeding cars. So even though we were getting pictures of the person we were after, the pictures weren't of high enough quality for the general to act. I asked the colonel for another twenty-four hours, which he granted us, and we went to work devising new plans to address this technical shortfall. We were in a location where we couldn't exactly stand up and conduct a brainstorming session with flip charts. We huddled under our makeshift camouflage of branches and tarps, used a small waterproof notebook, and whispered different ideas back and forth between us. We didn't differentiate between experienced teammates and newbies like Cappy. You were either a teammate or you weren't. Cappy's contribution counted just as much as everyone else's, and that was a good thing, because his idea saved the mission.

Cappy's idea was to dig a pothole in the road our target's car would be using. The driver would have to slow down and take a wide turn to avoid the pothole, thus giving us the opportunity to get a better shot of the target. We used our night-vision goggles, infrared lights, squad radios, and an E-tool (entrenching shovel) with two two-man pothole teams; one team dug while the other team monitored traffic. We worked all night to get the initial pothole dug and then practiced taking pictures of other cars during the day to see if they slowed enough for the autofocus to work. The good news was that after the first night, the pothole did a good enough job to convince Colonel Stones not to abort the mission. Each night we worked on our pothole a little more. Eight days later, we got the pictures our general was looking for; shortly thereafter, Doctor Death was captured and brought to The Hague to stand trial for war crimes. Though we were just one part of a multifaceted mission to apprehend the war criminal, Colonel Stones was so pleased with the outcome of the mission that he awarded us Army Commendation and Achievement Medals for our actions. (It's unusual for one service branch to grant medals to another branch.)

When a SEAL platoon returns from an overseas deployment, the officer in charge (OIC—in this case that was me) hosts a debriefing session for all SEALs of the team. These debriefs are a powerful way to share lessons learned so other teammates can be better prepared when they deploy into harm's way. When I discussed this mission, I specifically called out how we debated the different options and highlighted Cappy's mission-saving idea. How do you think it made him feel? How do you think the other newbies about to be deployed felt when they heard that the new guy had had the best idea? Guess what happens when people feel that their contributions and their opinions are respected. They feel empowered to contribute more. The job of a leader is to get the best contributions from his teammates and to help them dig deeper and give more of themselves for the team. Like building trust and setting direction, respect is habit-forming.

PLAYING AND PULLING WITH CARE

Ask any sports fan to name the most successful sports teams in history, and most will immediately respond with an answer that includes a pro team: the Yankees, Patriots, Lakers, Bulls, and Celtics would all sit high atop any such list. It is easy to understand their response because pro teams get most of the television exposure. But the most successful teams of all time aren't always the most famous ones. To the knowledgeable sports fanatic, John Wooden's UCLA basketball teams are the gold standard of sports success. In twelve years, Wooden's teams won ten NCAA titles, including a remarkable seven in a row. No team since has won more than two consecutively. Coach Wooden (1910–2010) often spoke about his coaching philosophy. He thought of himself as a teacher, and along with a focus on getting his team into top condition, he wanted his players to experience peace of mind—knowing that they'd given their best efforts;

he also celebrated them as team players, not as individual superstars.

Though he spoke in detail about building championship teams, there is one topic he never discussed with his teams: winning. He didn't want his teams focused on winning; he wanted them focused on giving their best efforts for the team, respecting each other, and eliminating ego from play. He reminded his players constantly, "Much can be accomplished by teamwork when no one is concerned about who gets credit."[5]

No college team before or after Coach Wooden has replicated his teams' performances. There are a host of runners-up in the world of basketball, however, such as Coach Geno Auriemma of UConn and Coach Pat Summitt of Tennessee, both of whom led their women's programs on record-setting championship runs. Auriemma and Summitt are worth including in the conversation because they subscribed to the same formula for success that Coach Wooden deployed: connection, achievement, respect, empowerment.

It might sound trite to practice the principles of CARE and to use words like *love*, *respect*, and *truth* in the context of business, but it's trite only if you don't sincerely embrace these principles in every action you take—if you don't embody them as a leader, as a team member, and as an organization. If your words match your actions, you can't fail. And neither can your team. Ask someone who has been a member of an unstoppable team—whether a basketball player, an executive committee member, or a Navy SEAL—and you'll hear the same thing: we won not because we feared losing; we won because we didn't want to disappoint one another.

There's a misconception that the best coaches are the meanest, the loudest screamers, or the smartest strategists. Not true. Though good play calling is certainly helpful, just as good business decisions and smart strategies help businesses prosper, what separates the average from the awesome teams are coaches who hold their players accountable for their actions on and off the field; they know that caring for your teammates is a 24/7 commitment. The greater the care you show as a leader, the greater the care your players (and your teammates) will show for the team's goals. If all players give it their all—this is the "peace of mind" Coach Wooden refers to—then they know they cannot fail and that their team will support them. They play out of joy, not fear.

This kind of talk may sound utopian, perhaps even slightly spiritual. You know what? It is! Consider the football program at De La Salle High School in Concord, California. It set the national record for the most consecutive wins at 151. They were undefeated from 1992 to 2004, more than doubling the previous record of 72 wins in a row. Their coach, Bob Ladouceur, said the secret to their success was creating an environment where love powered the game plan for perfect effort. No doubt Coach Ladouceur and his staff were good at calling plays and understanding their competition, but the difference maker was their authentic commitment to each other. Ladouceur demanded that all players "give perfect effort from start to finish." And they would, because he and his coaches viewed their teams not as groups of athletes but as family members.

Players who became boastful of their own skills and sought personal recognition were sidelined and even banished if they didn't change their selfish ways to embrace the selflessness required for team success. Coach Ladouceur wasn't into coaching perfect seasons for his own glory, and he didn't use those accomplishments as a springboard for higher-paying coaching opportunities, though he had plenty of offers. Instead, he chose to set the example of humility that he expected his players to embrace. He knew that his "kids" were observant and that his actions and the actions of his coaches set the example for his teams. In his book on Ladouceur and the De La Salle Spartans, *When the Game Stands Tall*, journalist Neil Hayes quoted the coach thus:

> Kids respect true humility and that you stand for something more than winning. . . . They will fight for you and your program if you stand for more than that. It boils down to what you believe in as a person, and I'm talking about how life should be lived

and people should be treated. Kids see all that. It's a whole package of things that have nothing to do with standing in front of a team with a piece of chalk. You can know who to block and what play to call, but it has no meaning unless the kids know who you are. Our kids aren't fighting for wins. They're fighting for a belief in what we stand for.[6]

Off the field, Ladouceur taught a religion class. Like John Wooden, he wanted to school his students in life skills. Like all unstoppable leaders, these two coaches sought a higher purpose; winning was a by-product of perfect effort on the playing field and in life.

Consider another highly successful high school football coach, Joe Ehrmann. Coach Ehrmann is a former NFL Pro Bowl defensive player who became a pastor and a coach for inner-city kids at Gilman School in Baltimore. His methodologies for coaching success are captured in the book *Season of Life*. He teaches his inner-city players how to care for each other so deeply that bonds of love are developed. These connections are so strong and are reinforced so consistently that players willingly give all they have, and more than they think they have, to play for each other. His focus on building teams is based on the ultimate expression of care: love.

Now consider a sport near and dear to my heart, the epitome of team sports: eight-oared rowing. The best teams row as one. There is no MVP (most valuable player), no highest scorer, and no runner with the most yards gained. Rowing in eights has just one objective: pulling perfectly in unison to go faster than the competition. The effort required to do this is physically demanding and downright painful. Exercise physiologists have equated the amount of physical exertion of elite, eight-oared rowing crews to playing two back-to-back professional basketball games. The pain is so intense during these five and a half minutes of exercise that rowers routinely faint at the end of the race. All the top rowing teams are well conditioned and technically skilled, but the great ones are also willing to embrace extreme physical discomfort. Why? Because they are in service to each other and to their shared goals.

Few sports teams have been as unstoppable as the US women's eight-oared rowing team. They won every single international competition, from World Championships (every year) to Olympic gold medals from 2006 to 2016. That's eleven consecutive world and Olympic gold medals. The only team to win more championships in the world was the Soviet-era Russian hockey team from the mid-1960s to the 1970s. And here's the surprise: unlike men's basketball or Soviet hockey teams, the women's rowing team didn't rely on returning stars to win season after season. In fact, only one rower consistently remained in the lineup for six of the eleven consecutive championships, Meghan Musnicki. The only other constant through those winning years was the coach, Tom Terhaar. Often considered an enigma for his quiet and reserved style of listening twice as much as he speaks, this father of four avoids the limelight and redirects the light to his athletes. In his words, "This isn't about me. Coaches don't get a medal."[7] When asked about Coach Terhaar's coaching style, Musnicki responded effusively: "He's an amazing coach. He's tough. He asks a lot of us and expects a lot from us, but it's all worth it. I wouldn't be here if I didn't trust him and if he didn't put his faith in me as an athlete."[8]

As it is for other unstoppable coaches, the hallmarks of Terhaar's approach are humility, a selfless work ethic, trust, respect, and pushing his athletes further than they originally thought possible. Susan Francia, a two-time Olympic gold medalist under Coach Terhaar, said, "He was tough, and at times I hated him, but I always respected him. He pushed me to my limits: to achievements of which I didn't know I was humanly capable. I truly believe we would never have won gold without him."[9]

Being a CARE-based leader doesn't mean being "soft" on your teammates. To the contrary, it means caring for them enough to push them to unlock their very best effort. For eleven years, Coach Terhaar has set the gold standard for this kind of unselfish excellence. As Katelin Snyder, a twenty-eight-year-old coxswain from Detroit, puts it, "You don't go fast by beating another girl. . . . You go fast by being your best self and bringing that girl with you."[10]

Mutual respect in team building is not about creating friendships, though don't be surprised when you develop friendships with people you openly show respect for; it's about recognizing contributions. Team building is a paradox of sorts, because you need different skill sets to succeed, yet success is found only through unity. The most powerful teams are the ones that have breadth of skill *and* depth of unity.

ACTING LIKE YOU MEAN IT

Being the boss, having an impressive title, and sitting at the top of the organizational chart will gain you only a thin veneer of respect from the members of your team. If your actions do not support your position of authority, you will be ineffective as a leader.

If you really want to be someone whom other people are willing to follow, you must be willing to let go of your own insecurities and fears. The respect you expect to receive from your team depends on your showing respect for them too. You must recognize your own limitations with an open heart while celebrating your team's contributions wholeheart-edly. A team leader's responsibility is not only to build trust and set direction, but also to create an environment of mutual respect, so teammates feel free to voice their opinions, debate options, and ultimately take actions without fear of ridicule. This is where the leader's true power and authority come from.

As a leader, it can be challenging not to take yourself too seriously and not to be blinded by ambition and power. Every leader, every human being, is susceptible to these temptations. However, great leaders find ways to keep these drives and urges in check, to not fall victim to disrespectful comments or actions that make them look good at the expense of their team. I know because I've been there too. We are prone to lashing out in an uncaring, disrespectful manner when we feel threatened or unsure of ourselves—exactly the kind of situation that unstoppable teams find themselves in all the time. We react too quickly and too sharply, or we jump to conclusions, allowing our emotions to take control, or we simply stop listening to what others are saying.

Leading a team can be stressful, and when under pressure, we may act in ways that make matters worse, triggering negative responses in others rather than defusing tense moments and building mutual respect. Leaders can be constant sources of strength for their teams or their teams' worst enemies. We have our emotions to thank for both of those outcomes. As neuroscience shows, our emotions can overwhelm us in ways both positive and negative, especially so when your team gives you bad news or the smell of failure is in the air. Here's one technique I've used to help me manage my emotions and avoid heat-of-the-moment reactions.

I force myself to stop talking, stand tall, and take three deep, controlled breaths. I breathe in for three seconds, hold for three seconds, and exhale for three seconds, asking a question at the end of each breath. I do not respond until I have heard the answers to these three questions. Sometimes I put these questions to myself; sometimes, to those around me; sometimes both:

1. What happened?
2. What were you trying to achieve?
3. What are you going to do about it?

Remember, your team's personality is a reflection of the team leader's personality. If you allow your emotions to cloud your judgment, if you snap back without first seeking to understand the whole picture, you are setting the wrong mood. By remaining calm (that's what deep breathing can help you with) and by asking questions to help you understand what's going on, what challenges the team faces—what negative emotions and fears they may be confronting—you will help the team feel respected, and they will feel safe enough to share vital information with you that may save your mission from failure. As the leader, your actions are always under review; you are constantly being observed by your teammates. How you handle yourself during the most trying times (failure, a great struggle, or both) is the measure of your leadership. When in doubt: breathe, ask, and repeat!

C.A.R.E. Loop

CHAPTER 6

EMPOWER

In the 1970s, the Recording Industry Association of America followed the three-decade practice of individual record companies by introducing sales-recognition levels named after precious metals to recognize the most popular albums. A gold record was awarded to an artist whose album sold five hundred thousand units; platinum was reserved for albums that exceeded a million units in sales. The fitness industry doesn't have a sales award system like this. Veterans just call a hit product a grand slam or a hundred-year storm or simply say, "You got lucky." However, there's a term in both industries for a successful artist or company that comes out of nowhere, dominates for a season, and then fades away into oblivion—a "one-hit wonder." Whether you're a recording artist or high-tech entrepreneur, having a one-hit wonder is great, but repeating it is even better.

When the Perfect Pushup became a breakout success, nothing irked me more than being called a one-hit-wonder entrepreneur. If the Perfect Pushup had been an album, it would have received multiple platinum awards within its first year. What it got instead was a whole host of comments from industry veterans saying, in essence, "Enjoy it while you can. You got lucky, kid." Yet over the next eight years, five more of our products—Perfect Pullup, Perfect Multi-Gym, Perfect Ab Carver, Perfect Cooling Towel, and Perfect Smartphone Armband—earned the equivalent of platinum status, and several others sold at gold level. No longer could someone say, "You got lucky, kid." That's because we had created a system for developing products that sold in the millions. What was the secret of the team behind these series of successes? Empowerment.

Our products didn't come from one inventive genius; they came from the entire team. Every single person on the team owned the product-idea process. When people are owners, they think cooperatively. They share ideas, test new concepts, and focus on finding the best idea no matter who comes up with it. They act *selflessly*. Put simply, empowerment, which closes the CARE loop, depends on three actions: educate, enable, and engage.

It's important to point out that the CARE loop isn't a linear sequence; it's a virtuous circle, an infinite series of repeatable actions that build on and depend on the other actions in the loop. As soon as you've empowered people, you need to turn your attention to renewing the connection that fueled your team's unstoppable momentum. Teams come together to accomplish specific goals. When the effort is done, they may disband or be reconstituted in membership for the sake of new goals, so you must keep renewing the bonds that tie them together. This is a healthy, natural process; it's good not only for people on the team, but also for the organization itself.

To empower people is to give them responsibility *and* authority. This may sound like a fine line of demarcation, but it's a significant distinction in the team-building process. Giving people the authority to make decisions without being forced to check in with the boss for approval opens the way for them to start thinking of themselves as owners, not employees. They, too, must embrace the CARE loop in their dealings with others. The CARE loop helps keep your current team aligned, inspired, and empowered, but ideally it becomes a tool that all members use to empower themselves and take on bigger leadership roles.

Nothing shows people you care more than dedicating time to helping them learn new skills. Be careful, however: *telling* people what you know (and what they *don't* know) isn't the same as *teaching* them. Empowerment isn't a task you can check off your list or test on paper; it develops over time and depends on creating an environment where every person on the team shares lessons learned and feels a responsibility to coach and support other team members' growth. Like everything else, it begins and ends with you, the leader of the team. In a sense, you stand in the center of the CARE loop, keeping it spinning and the team's momentum going. Then it becomes everyone's responsibility to create CARE loops, each nurturing the loop and seeking new ways to get the job done. That's empowerment.

THE GEOMETRY OF EDUCATION

Think of education as a triangle. Each side of the triangle expresses one of the three ways to educate someone, and ideally you want to be creating an equilateral triangle in which all three sides are equal. Here's how I define each one:

- **LEAPFROGGING**: This is in-house and often informal training delivered via lessons learned, best practices, debriefings, or e-mail updates shared among teammates.
- **EXTERNALITY**: This tends to be more formal training provided by outside professionals, often representing unusual or diverse fields of expertise.
- **ON-THE-JOB TRAINING (OJT)**: On-the-job training gives people the chance to put their knowledge to work. This

learning-by-doing approach may include mentoring and coaching as well.

When you create a system for educating your teammates with all three sides of the triangle, they will develop the "know what," the "know why," and the "know how" to achieve goals and develop new confidence and capabilities for future roles. All too often, leaders outsource training to third parties, focusing only on external sources, which can be useful but don't prepare teams for OTH goals. To be sure, external education is an important part of empowerment, but only if the other two sides of the triangle are equally well developed. Leapfrogging and OJT are just as valuable. Indeed, it's dedication to all three types of education, not one at the expense of the others, that empowers your team.

When I was leading SEAL Team platoons, we spent twelve to eighteen months preparing for overseas missions. (Training schedules have accelerated since then, due to changes in operations.) During predeployment training, almost half of our training time was dedicated to skill-specific schools, such as sniper training, jump mastery, or combat diving. However, we also engaged in less obviously germane training programs intended to expand our perspectives and insights and thus increase team members' capabilities and confidence. Among them were civilian schools run by former Las Vegas showmen, Olympians, and NASCAR drivers. Part of what makes a SEAL Team so successful is the focus on unconventional warfare training and on a learning process that supports unconventional thinking. The Las Vegas showman who could shoot playing cards out of the sky showed us the art of rapid target acquisition. The Olympian showed us how to swim faster and more efficiently in the water. The NASCAR driver showed our drivers how to use a car as both a weapon and a blocking force.

SEAL platoons are in a continuous learning loop. Platoon commanders and their assistant platoon commanders are there for a relatively short time—eighteen to twenty-four months. The senior enlisted leadership staff are on similar cycles of rotation. Training the next generation is paramount to keeping SEAL Team competitive in the world of asymmetrical warfare. Investing in our younger, less experienced teammates' education not only improves their confidence and capabilities but also empowers them to participate in providing thoughtful input in mission planning and execution. The old saying "A chain is only as strong as its weakest link" is apropos to team building. That's why in SEAL platoons the most experienced members get paired with the least experienced ones. The smallest team is a team of two; in SEAL Team we call this a swim pair. When newbies arrive, they're paired with more knowledgeable and experienced teammates. The idea is to reduce the knowledge gap by rapidly educating the newest members and hence strengthening the weakest links. Educating each other is everyone's responsibility. A lesson learned is not truly learned until it is shared and taught to your teammates.

LEAPFROGGING

Do you recall the leapfrog game you played as a child during gym class? Each team would form a line in which each person would stand two arm lengths from those before and after them. Then all but the first leaper would kneel on all fours, and the last person in line would jump successively over each of the people in front. As each finished the jumps, he or she would yell out "Next" or the name of the next child in the line. It was a team race that could be won only by making sure that everyone jumped off the back of the person in front. The kind of education I'm talking about is much like the game of leapfrog: the goal is to help you leap ahead with new information that lands you in a position to learn even more; when you do, your job is to return the favor by sharing your learning to help others leap ahead—an endless loop of learning.

When you have a leapfrog mentality, you will find it difficult to identify your weakest link, because people are continually educating one another. This educational mind-set allows SEALs and other special-operations units to be flexible in operating with a wide variety of team dynamics. For example, weeks before we went on a mission to Bosnia, the commanding officer of our forward-deployed unit presented me with two missions that were to occur simultaneously but in vastly different locations: Bosnia and the Congo. The Bosnian mission involved hunting a war criminal, while the Congo mission required helping a US embassy. Because of the timing of these two missions, we had to split our platoon into two smaller teams and add specialists, such as combat boat pilots and explosive-ordnance disposal (EOD) technicians. I went to Bosnia with an EOD specialist, while my chief petty officer went to the Congo with a special boat team to navigate the Congo River. He was empowered to tackle the task at hand, for he had the training, confidence, responsibility, and authority to complete the mission.

A word about chief petty officers: they have the most experience in SEAL Team. In most cases, they train the platoon commanders. That was certainly the case with me and my chief! He and I did routine check-ins to assess progress and share information on both missions. Our communication was not hierarchical; he wasn't reporting and asking for permission. We simply reported to each other what we were experiencing and learning. This type of "flat," or nonhierarchical, discussion can be difficult or impossible if trust, direction, and mutual respect have not been developed first.

When assessing which idea is best, egos need to be subdued so ideas can be objectively evaluated to decide on the best course of action. Subduing egos means assessing ideas on their merit without preference for rank or position.

Education is the first step in empowering people to go beyond the expected, but it requires active engagement from the leader. No sooner does someone return from an educational class in SEAL Team than their new learnings are used on a training mission. Snipers get to take shots, jumpmasters spot and send out jumpers, drivers lead convoys—and they do it all in front of their teammates. Three things happen when you let your teammates demonstrate their new skills to their peers: you build confidence, you build respect, and you encourage them all to keep developing their new skills.

LEARNING ON THE CLOCK

On-the-job training can occur only when people are given the responsibility to put to work what they've learned. In SEAL Team, our training mantra is "Train like you fight." OJT works the same way and is, I would argue, the best training you can give someone. However, OJT is only as good as your willingness as the leader to let go of control and pass it to your people. Your input and your teammates' feedback are critical components to making OJT effective. The distinction between internal education like leapfrogging and OJT is that leapfrogging is a communal sharing of lessons learned, while OJT is specifically to let a person take on new experiences and be held accountable for results, with plenty of opportunities for coaching and improvement along the way.

Some of the most challenging OJT sessions in SEAL platoon training are contact drills. This live-fire training is done using real bullets, not blanks, and it is inherently dangerous and intense. The basic concept behind contact drills is to train a platoon for all kinds of different enemy-engagement scenarios. Besides paying attention to one's field of fire (a person's area of shooting responsibility), everyone must be prepared to make a decision. Because you cannot control where an enemy engagement occurs, SEAL instructors will initiate contact drills where platoons are most vulnerable. The drill could start while you're crossing a river, road, or field or walking through a valley. It's everyone's responsibility to be on the lookout for enemy engagement. To make it more challenging, instructors will remove key decision makers, such as the platoon commander or the chief or leading petty officer, from the platoon to force others to step up and make decisions. In SEAL platoons, these moments are called down-man drills. These drills give every individual the experience of taking charge of the group's progress and safety. Talk about owning it! Every participant must step up at some point to lead the rest of the platoon. Not only do drills like this teach teams to develop empathy and respect for the challenges that go with calling the shots (literally, in this case), but they also put every team member in a position of authority so as to practice being ready to lead at a moment's notice. In the workplace, we don't have enemies shooting, but we do have competitors to contend with. We do face uncertainty, and we're likely to find ourselves in situations where teammates aren't available to fulfill their usual roles due to vacations, sabbaticals, or family leave. The best OJT programs give participants the opportunity to practice and improve in real time with real things at stake.

Shortly after I sold Perfect Fitness to a much larger company, Implus Corporation in Durham, North Carolina, I needed to build a new team. First on my list of new teammates was a salesperson. There was no budget to hire a new employee, so I was offered a list of existing employees in North Carolina from which to select a new team member. (Per terms of the sale, all back-end operations were moved to North Carolina, while sales, marketing, and product development stayed in California.) I didn't know anyone on the list, and I didn't have much time to decide. We were rapidly rolling out new products, and I desperately needed someone to help me carry the burden of traveling around the country. After speaking with a few people, I picked a young man who had a checkered past in sales. The senior leaders of the company recommended that I pick someone else, because they didn't think he was the right person for the job. They argued that he lacked experience, which he did, and that his personality—described as a know-it-all bordering on sheer arrogance—would annoy buyers and hence be a detriment to growing the Perfect Fitness line. I hadn't spent much time with my new salesman, Matt, but I saw some special qualities in his background. He had a hunger to learn new things, demonstrated a strong work ethic, and, more important, he seemed open to listening. I decided that I would give Matt six months to prove himself and prove his critics wrong. If it didn't work, I told the executives at my new company, then I promised to pick one of their other choices.

The first thing Matt and I did was go on a series of sales calls together. I included him in every phase of the sales call, from the e-mails I sent the buyers to putting together the sales presentations to brainstorming potential buyer questions and my responses. I gave him direct insight into how I approached a sales call, and I invited him into the meetings. I introduced him as my sales colleague and even encouraged him to field answers to client questions in sales meetings. We did three sales calls together. I ran the first one from start to finish. On the second one, he gave portions of the presentation, such as Implus's capabilities, which he knew better than I. On the third one, he did the main presentation, and I did backup. At the end of the third presentation, we went to lunch, and I walked him through all my critical feedback points. I started my conversation with him just the way my infomercial director would speak to me when giving me a critique: "It's not personal. I just want the best performance." Matt heard the good, the bad, and the ugly of his presentation. I discussed with him all kinds of seemingly small details that impeded his ability to build trust with the buyer.

Matt and I spent two hours going over my feedback. We role-played how to take actions different from the ones he'd used during that meeting. I wasn't critical in a negative way, but I was critically constructive in educating him as to how to be a better salesman. I still remember that day vividly, because at the end of the two hours he looked at me and said, "No one has ever taken the time to explain this to me. Thank you." He was genuinely grateful for the feedback, and it showed. We got into a routine of discussing each sales call like a mission briefing. Remember, we were three thousand miles apart, so communication was paramount. We had three simple stages to discuss, and they paralleled mission planning: sales prep, the actual meeting, and follow-up sales tasks. Similarly, basic SEAL mission planning is organized in three phases: insertion, actions on the objective, and extraction.

Guess what happened. He improved on every single sales "mission"; it was our version of contact drills! Our mindset was to always learn something new and avoid repeating a mistake. Over the next six months, Matt's sales growth was remarkable. I gave him regional accounts; we tracked progress, and he grew each one. We rang the bell (from California) while he was on speakerphone, announcing to the entire West Coast team the new accounts he'd landed.

As his sales responsibility grew, so did his education. To my knowledge, I was then the only sales rep in retail fitness who maintained an active personal-training certification. I figured that if I was selling fitness products, I should be a certified fitness trainer so I could help educate retail buyers, many of whom rotate into buying roles with very little knowledge about the fitness category. I earned my certification long before the Perfect Pushup came to market, and when it did, that fitness background was invaluable in helping buyers understand the finer points of product design and the functional benefits to their customers. Getting a certification is expensive and time-consuming and requires yearly off-site training, and I thought it would be the perfect next step in Matt's empowerment journey as a salesman. Matt's performance spoke for itself. Every account he was responsible for had grown by double digits, and some had exploded, doubling in sales, as he built trusting relationships with key buyers. Better still, he was eager to spend the extra hours to earn his personal-training certification. His confidence grew by the week. Four months later, he passed his final exams to earn his certificate.

What do you think happened next? Matt got better, more confident, and even maybe a little arrogant from time to time, but he was a different person from the one I'd met three years earlier. The executives at Implus noticed his performance improvement too. In those three years, he grew our sales team, helped hire new people, and eventually took over as the head of sales for Perfect Fitness.

I offer this story not to thump my own chest but to demonstrate the power of educating, enabling, and engaging your teammates. The time you spend with them—focused just on them—demonstrates how much you care about them and their success. I often told Matt that I was grooming him to replace me. He would balk at the thought and ask, "How can I replace the founder of the company?"

"Simple," I'd say. "Be better at the job than he is."

Matt didn't believe in himself to that extent at that moment, but I did, and I proved my belief in him by fighting to educate him, enable him with resources, and then engage with him on what he learned and how he was using his resources. By the end, we did our own form of down-man drills. I was tagging along on *his* sales calls and watching (and learning from) him. Matt was empowered and, because he was, he moved mountains.

CLOSING THE LOOP

As a team leader, you are the person who closes the loop, builds a bridge between team members, and helps them stay on track. You will use a host of different techniques (communication, aspiration, assessments, recognition, goal setting, educating, etc.), but the intention behind your actions remains the same: to empower them to go far beyond their limits—and frequently yours, too. Creating a culture of empowerment can be challenging, because it requires the leader to let go, to relinquish control so that others can step up, make decisions, and take control as well. For those who are insecure, proud, egotistical, or selfish, sharing one's power is a foreign and terrifying concept. However, here's the irony: the more you empower others, the more the power returns to you. It comes back to you in a different, even more potent form: gratitude. As a leader, your role is to grow your people to achieve their highest potential. Each phase of the CARE loop builds upon the others, and this final phase completes a group's transformation from selfishness to selflessness, from a group of individuals to an unstoppable team.

I suspect most of us have had the privilege to witness or benefit from an extraordinary act by someone we know, something that goes above and beyond what is required and what is called for. Most of us can't help but admire these people and be grateful for their selfless acts. All too often, though, such acts aren't acknowledged by team leaders, much less celebrated. That's why empowerment is such a fragile resource. It grows steadily under the right conditions, but it withers quickly when teammates view achievement and rewards as scarce resources that must be hoarded. You want to be a leader who spreads the love and recognition around, not one who parcels it out sparingly. Only then will you be building a team, not a collection of self-interested career climbers.

We all have strengths and weaknesses, yet some are celebrated more than others; they just tend to stand out from everyone else. Superstars can be intoxicating to work with, because they appear to be game changers on whatever real or metaphorical field they compete. This is often the case in team sports such as basketball and soccer, where the entire team may be constructed around the talents of one or two superstars who get all the attention, perks, and financial rewards. The rest of the team seems to exist only to enable the superstar to achieve greatness. This construct works well in our media-frenzied world, where selling jerseys and sporting memorabilia is critical for maintaining a profitable sports franchise. The same dynamic can be found in financial services (the star trader or stock picker), medicine (the leading surgeon), and startups (the entrepreneur/inventor).

However, consider how well that works over time—not so well. Think Enron, Lehman Brothers, Theranos, or perhaps even Tesla. Adding a star to your team may be necessary in some instances, but wouldn't it be better if every member of the team possessed the skills and sensibilities required for success? How many times have you watched a superstar's team come up short in a championship? In the corporate world, how many times have we seen a supposed genius burn out and blow up his entire company?

Star-driven teams can offer a quick fix, but all too often they end up causing long-term headaches. Why? They are not built on selflessness and empowerment, but just the opposite. Hard to build, but more durable in the end, are teams on which everyone owns the results and feels empowered to pursue their best efforts—to find true peace of mind through emotional connection, achievement, respect, and empowerment, just as Coach Wooden inspired his players to do.

People admire those who can bound over buildings, sizzle on the big screen, or win over boardrooms with their charisma. Bright stars tend to burn out quickly, however, leaving the others lulled into complacency and cynicism. Worse, the others may leave in search of a team environment that will nurture their talents and give them the chance to go all in. History shows that superstars are no match for empowered teams.

A revealing example of empowerment can be found in General Stanley McChrystal's book *Team of Teams*. In recounting his growth as a leader, he refers to "his day of reckoning"—the day he realized he was the choke point for his team; he was holding them back because the system he operated in required his leaders to seek his approval before making a mission decision. This process was the classic military command-and-control hierarchy, wherein information flows up to a decision maker and then his decision flows back down through the ranks to the fighter on the battlefield. The enemy, in this case terrorists, didn't have these same decision-making constraints; they were essentially making their own battlefield decisions, which made them more agile, faster to act and to retreat. The very organizational structure that had historically enabled the US military to dominate the battlefield was now proving to be a liability. As the commander of Joint Special Operations Command (JSOC), General McChrystal measured how many missions were conducted per month. When he first took command of JSOC in 2003, an average of sixteen special-operations missions were conducted per month seeking terrorists in Iraq and Afghanistan. The enemies were executing three times as many missions per month, and their operations were decentralized, with local leaders empowered to create and execute missions at will.

No doubt US military personnel had better training and

better equipment, but they weren't as empowered *to act* as the enemy was. To turn the tide against the terrorists, General McChrystal took a major risk. He broke away from traditional command-and-control protocol and began sharing sensitive, compartmentalized information with over seven thousand special operators and their support teams. He created a daily update of the latest information and shared it across the globe on closed-circuit video feeds. Once his team knew what he knew, he enabled them to execute missions more quickly by changing the chain of command required for mission approval, essentially pushing decision-making responsibility down to the level of lieutenant colonels. That's a drop of five ranks! His rationale was simple: his leaders now had the same knowledge he had, *and* they were much closer to the battlefield. Still, he didn't give them carte blanche to conduct any mission they wanted. He instituted a daily engagement section of his briefings, with various battlefield commanders leading the briefings. This opened the door to openly engaging with them. Engagement wasn't focused on the "who" as much as on the "what" and the "how." Priority one was sharing what was working and what wasn't and how to make the missions more successful.

General McChrystal considered his role to be that of a gardener, whose job it is to constantly be weeding and pruning to enable the plants (his leaders) to grow and thrive. Missions per month soared to over three hundred. In this new empowered structure, McChrystal's teams were completing missions in one night that would have taken them a month to complete in the past. More important, they were now making a positive impact on the battlefield. Information flowed so well that special-operations teams were able not only to respond faster but also to predict where the enemy would strike next. By the time General McChrystal left his post in 2008, his "team of teams" had amassed a remarkable success rate in reducing the number of terrorists on the battlefield.

Moreover, empowerment isn't reserved for just making decisions. The dizzying pace of innovation has caused organizations to rethink how to embrace change and innovate faster. In much the same way that McChrystal grappled with a decentralized, empowered, and well-armed enemy, today's corporations deal with similar challenges. Enemies are called competitors and are mostly the small, empowered, and highly skilled startups that are redefining the business landscape. With the advent of high-speed networks and wireless connected devices, there is now more data and information available than ever before. No longer is gaining access and analyzing information the choke point to innovation; instead the stranglehold is an organization's structure.

At Great Place to Work's 2017 For All Summit in Chicago, the former executive chairman and CEO of Cisco John

Chambers explained that the near ubiquity of Internet-connected devices will only increase, from seventeen billion in 2017 to a projected five hundred billion in 2027, adding, "You're going to have information coming into your company in ways you never imagined before. . . . Decisions will be made much further down in the organization at a fast pace."[1]

This is the same challenge General McChrystal faced on the battlefield. He overcame it by empowering his team leaders with the responsibility and authority to make decisions. That same change will be required on corporate teams. The consulting firm Great Place to Work recently published a research paper that defines how organizations will need to adapt to the coming explosion of connected devices and the data and analyses that will flow through them. Its suggestion is simple: get everyone innovating! Unfortunately, the researchers could identify few examples of companies that were empowering their teams to make those changes.

How do you think these organizations can get everyone to participate in innovation? How do they, as the report puts it, "maximize a company's human potential by tapping into the intelligence, skills, and passion of everyone in the organization"? They do it by building relationships with their employees in which trust, direction, respect, and empowerment aren't optional but mandatory. Great Place to Work calls this ideal innovation by all. I call it empowerment.

Throughout this book, I've emphasized that the CARE loop is a never-ending process that is elemental for unstoppable teams. In the next chapter, I want to help you expand the definition of a team by looking at all the constituents and stakeholders outside of the immediate team who can influence, contribute to, and, yes, empower your mission. No team operates in a vacuum, and no team achieves greatness without the help of others.

C.A.R.E. Loop

CHAPTER 7

ACTIVATING THE 10X ADVANTAGE

The previous four chapters addressed how to lead with CARE to build unstoppable teams. Now it's time to broaden the team-building discussion to include other constituents and stakeholders who have a hand in your team's success or might be affected by your team's performance. One of the risks of a single-minded, insular focus on the workings of your team is that you lose perspective on how others might hurt or harm your team's progress. The definition of *team* might be bigger than you realize at first.

You may not be aware that less than 1 percent of the US population serves in the military today, but they're not the only ones serving America. The military depends on millions of civilian hands and minds, from those who make uniforms, meals, and equipment to those developing the scientific and technological breakthroughs that keep the military personnel safe. No team can do it alone, whether you're conducting a mission or creating new products. In fact, when a team authentically proves how much they care about other people, they experience an exponential return on their efforts, which I call the 10x advantage.

This 10x advantage can be found on the battlefield, in business, and in communities. In business, the 10x advantage is routinely found in companies where a small team takes on an outsize and much better funded opponent. I personally have experienced the 10x advantage in SEAL Team, startups, nonprofits, and community action groups where small numbers of people realized huge gains in comparison to their size. In each circumstance, the 10x advantage was activated by aligning the actions of the internal team with the goals and actions of external allies.

SERVE SOMEBODY

Consider the fictional story of Hunter and Brooke, who were born in the same year on a coastal wooded island where they attended the same schools. When they graduated, both decided to become home builders. The island they lived on had very strict building codes, so the houses they built were similar in outward appearance. Getting customers was tough, because both built the same products and everyone on the island knew how much a home cost, so Hunter and Brooke couldn't compete on price.

When they started their businesses, Hunter immediately had more prospective customers than Brooke, thanks to his popularity in school. He had been the star quarterback for the school football team and had been voted "most likely to succeed" in his graduating class. He was outgoing and charismatic, loved to promote himself, and had a large group of friends. Brooke, on the other hand, had run on the cross-country team, was reserved, and had only a handful of friends. She spent her free time exploring the forests of the island, sketching, and doing woodworking. Hunter and Brooke were opposites in every way except for their professions. When people heard that both had become home builders, it seemed obvious to everyone that Hunter would be the one to succeed.

Hunter's reputation carried over to his business. He told everyone who would listen how much better his houses were than Brooke's. He hired people who didn't mind working in the shadow of his larger-than-life personality. He liked it that way, selecting people who made him feel good about himself and who did only what he told them to do. He made sure to let them know that they were the lucky ones who got to work with the best builder on the island. When he met with his customers, he did most of the talking, reminding them how good he was and why they should just follow his plans for their home. Hunter insisted that customers always meet at his office, whose walls were adorned with Hunter's various framed awards and citations. He wanted them to see how accomplished he was. His attitude was the same when selecting vendors. He believed that employees and vendors served him, not the other way around. When the community asked him to volunteer some of his time to work on local building projects, he always declined, claiming he was just too busy.

Brooke's approach was different. She focused on what she called the art of home building. She knew there were lots of skilled people who knew more than she did about how to build sturdy seaside homes. To her, building a home was a three-dimensional puzzle that involved location, local ecology, and the customer's needs. When she met with prospective customers, she always visited them at the site where they wanted to build their home. She listened more than she spoke, and when she did speak, she was usually asking a question. When she hired people, she looked for those who had a true passion for some element of the home-building process. She hired a sculptor who loved working with stone, a modeler whose hobby was building wooden schooners inside wine bottles, a Native American nicknamed the Tree Whisperer because he handpicked the trees for the lumber mill, and a landscaper who always *tasted* the dirt before deciding what to plant. Hunter joked about Brooke's employees, often calling them her "fruits and nuts."

Their different approaches to working with people resulted in different outcomes. When Hunter wasn't talking about himself, he was complaining about the lack of good vendors and quality employees. He often remarked that if it weren't for him, his vendors would be out of business. He found fault with their services and often threatened to replace them with off-island suppliers. He rarely spoke to them, but when he did, he always asked some variant of the same question: "What have you done for me lately?" He made his office staff push for vendor discounts and find ways to penalize them for even the most minor delays. He treated his employees no differently. They worked for *him*. Likewise, he always had problems keeping good builders. Hunter was constantly having to find replacements for workers who left of their own accord or were deemed "losers" by Hunter and fired. Frequently, Hunter resorted to hiring workers who'd never lived on the island, were unaware of his reputation, and knew little about seaside building techniques.

Brooke approached these relationships altogether differently. She visited vendor offices, getting to know their operations and the people who worked directly with her coworkers. She viewed her vendors as an extension of her team and made it her business to know the health of theirs. She never complained about her vendors. Indeed, she never missed an opportunity to thank them for delivering the products she needed. She treated them just like her coworkers, as part of her home-building team. On one occasion, the vendor who supplied her lumber suffered a catastrophic fire that wiped out available inventory. Determined not to let her supplier go out of business, Brooke prepaid her next lumber order to help keep their business alive, even as Hunter complained of the inconvenience and switched to an off-island vendor.

Brooke was even more committed to her employees, whom she referred to as artisans or craftsmen. She knew she'd never be as good as they were in their specialized skills, but she loved learning from them and encouraged them to learn from others, whether inside the company or off-island. Brooke was constantly looking for ways to help further develop and enrich her artisans' skills. Not surprisingly, she had very little employee turnover, and when she did say good-bye to a coworker, it was usually because she had helped them find their dream job. She realized that her business wasn't everyone's ideal job but that it could be a stepping-stone for the next one, and she was happy to play that role as long as her coworkers committed to her interests the way she committed to theirs.

When working with the community, Brooke's style was the opposite of Hunter's. She encouraged her craftsmen to participate in community projects and rarely turned one down. She personally designed the town's gazebo, and two of her artisans built it on their time off, completing it, to the delight of the community, faster than expected. She and her employees also helped renovate the town boathouse, which was used for all kinds of community efforts, from teaching kids to sail to holding boatbuilding workshops. She often told her people, "Our community is like a garden. The more we tend it, the more it will give back to us." She backed up her gardening philosophy by starting a yearly tradition of planting cedar seedlings to renew the island's cedar forest. She couldn't afford to pay her coworkers to do this, nor did she require them to join her on the first Saturday of spring. Most did anyway. She loved this springtime tradition. Word spread, and Brooke was joined by many of her vendors, schoolkids, and numerous townspeople.

Speaking of traditions, each of these two builders had different ways of celebrating the completion of a new house. Hunter's house celebrations were lavish affairs, and he'd lead everyone on a house tour, which gave him the opportunity to showcase his excellent work. Brooke's parties were simpler "key ceremonies." Unlike Hunter, who hired a catering company, Brooke and her coworkers hosted these ceremonies themselves, serving homemade appetizers and drinks. Her craftspeople took turns explaining their roles in building the house. Her tours ended with Brooke introducing the new homeowners to the vendors and office staff involved in creating the house. When Brooke spoke, it was never about herself; instead she praised the artisans she had the privilege to work with. The key ceremony always ended the same way: her Tree Whisperer would lead a native ritual that blessed the home and its occupants for good health and happiness. At the end of it, the woodworker would open his toolbox to produce a small cedar box that he'd hand to Brooke. She'd explain that each person involved in the building had signed the outside of the box. Inside were the keys to the house. As she'd hand the box to the new owner, she'd add, "From our hands to yours. We were honored to build your house. Now it's your turn to make it your home." These ceremonies frequently ended with hugs and a few tears of joy as clients, vendors, and artisans alike celebrated the new house.

From time to time, Hunter would hear of Brooke's key ceremonies or cedar-seedling tradition and immediately would call them a waste of time or assert that his events were better. Truth be told, neither the key ceremony nor the springtime planting day was Brooke's idea. Those ideas and many others had come from her artisans. Brooke was always quick to acknowledge these contributions and to express her willingness to learn from others and experiment with new ideas. When one of the ideas failed, she was quick to note, "A failure isn't a failure if we learn from it."

Gradually, Hunter had more and more trouble attracting new customers while Brooke's business grew so dramatically that she had a waiting list. At first she didn't understand why she had such an influx of customers, because she didn't advertise. Most of her new clients came through word-of-mouth referrals—from homeowners, vendors, craftspeople, and members of the community.

After a while, she had ten projects to Hunter's one. His only customers came from off-islanders in a rush for a new house. Not only did Brooke have more customers, but they also wanted people to know that their house had been built by Brooke and her team. That's ironic, because Hunter started his business as Hunter's Homes, while Brooke called hers Coastal Homes. Once people got to know Brooke and her team, they liked letting others know that theirs was a Brooke home. That phrase was used so often that Brooke reluctantly changed the name of her company, but only after her artisans surprised her one Christmas with a carved sign: COASTAL HOMES BY BROOKE BUILDERS. One customer asked Brooke in front of a couple of her artisans what it meant to be a Brooke builder. She blushed and was at a loss for words. Her craftspeople responded in unison: "It means we build with heart."

Hunter couldn't understand why his business, after showing such promise, was failing while Brooke's was blasting off. After all, their products were similar. Why was Brooke's business so unstoppable? Why was it ten times more successful than Hunter's?

EXPANDING THE CIRCLE

The point of this story is obvious: unstoppable teams are built on relationships, but not only the expected relationships with those directly in your line of sight and authority. It's also worth noting that the best team builders aren't necessarily extroverts—the "popular people." Great team builders may be loud and charismatic, but they are just as likely to be introverts with more reflective styles of communication.

The Hunters of the world expect relationships to be one-way streets. The Brookes see relationships as freeways with multiple lanes that go in both directions and have many entrances for other relationships. Brooke's approach to team building—her use of the CARE loop in all her dealings and with all stakeholders—created the 10x advantage. She understood that her team's success depended on expanding the definition of a team to include not just her employees, but also three other groups of stakeholders: customers, contributors (suppliers and vendors), and the community (the townspeople, schools, and local organizations that made this seaside location vibrant). Like Brooke, when you authentically extend the boundaries of your team to include your customers, contributors, and community, you exponentially increase your odds of success. When others feel a connection to your team, even if they may not be the ones swinging the hammers, pulling the triggers, or making the sales, what do you think happens? They willingly work harder to help you succeed because they know that when you succeed, they succeed—because they're a part of the team.

Helping those who help you sounds logical, right? However, the problem with common sense is it's not all that commonly applied, especially when egos, fortune, and fame are at stake. Whether your team-building focus is on scoring points or achieving returns on investment, the natural tendency is to focus on quick wins, because longer-term goals require deeper thinking, different perspectives, and sometimes bold steps out of one's comfort zone. Many teams become one-dimensional and imbalanced when the relationship with one constituency, usually the customer, is emphasized over others. Then team-building goals and resources are devoted to whomever and whatever can help hit the bull's-eye, and everyone and everything else becomes nonessential.

The problem with this "customer is everything" approach is that it disregards 67 percent of your other key teammates, who can help you get more customers. Startups are notorious for prioritizing this customer-centric approach. I get it. I have led startups, and I understand how critically important getting customers is. However, the brute-force method of acquiring customers at the start of a venture isn't likely to be sustainable over the long haul. If you want to grow and scale your business, you must engage all external teammates, not just current customers. The three constituents outside your organization—customers, contributors, and community—can become a force multiplier for your team's efforts. And when you bring them into the CARE loop, you'll see what it's like to be part of something bigger and better than any one team can achieve on its own.

In 1965, Bruce Tuckman published a theory of teams that described five stages of development or evolution that every team goes through.[1] His theory defined the transformation of a group of individuals into a team focused on a collective goal. It's a useful theory, and I agree with his general findings, but in my own experience, the theory doesn't go far enough. The challenge is that groups of individuals are often confused with a team. But unstoppable teams are more than just odds-and-ends collections of individuals thrown together due to proximity or background. As I've illustrated throughout the book, unstoppable teams are emotionally committed to each other and to ambitious goals. Still, it's easy to get stuck early in the process and think you've arrived at a "good enough" team. Sadly, that's what most people are accustomed to and that's why so many teams are such sorry, cynical cases of complacency. If you're starting to find yourself getting too comfortable with your efforts, I say: not so fast.

In my view, the transformation from a group of individuals to an unstoppable team is marked by five phases. Most leaders never take their team past the first step. Don't be one of those.

Here's how I define the five phases. You will notice that I do not include the dissolution of a team. I will return to that topic at the end of this chapter, for there is a right way and lots of wrong ways to disband a team.

- **PHASE 1: CONNECTED GROUP.** Activating a group of individuals through basic elements of connection is the starting point for everything else. Wannabe leaders sometimes think that by disseminating information through e-mails and holding mandatory meetings where they provide live updates, they are actually communicating and leading a team. In this phase, connections are still weak, and communication is impersonal; the leader does most of the talking and speaks mostly in terms of "I" and "me." Leaders tend to micromanage their direct reports, and direct reports focus mostly on "managing up." As you might guess, empowerment is nonexistent.

- **PHASE 2: DIRECTED GROUP.** The second team-building phase starts to turn the group's attention to goals identified by the team leader. This is not what I mean by unstoppable leadership. Telling someone to do something is not leading; it's managing. I have yet to find someone who says, "I love to be managed!" Directed groups are connected through an authoritarian figure who spends most of his time telling others what to do and how to do it. The direction is known, measurable, and achievable. Fear of failure is high, and people tend to focus only on the specific tasks they've been assigned. Information is disseminated on a need-to-know basis. Accountability is low, and the group's focus is on pleasing the leader and not being singled out for mistakes.

- **PHASE 3: RESPECTED TEAM.** Now we're starting to get somewhere. In this phase of team development, individuals have begun to feel emotionally connected to each other and to identify with the emerging team. They have started to feel intellectually invested in the group's progress toward achieving their goals. The group's leader, too, has started to shift gears, often seeking advice from the group, showing candor and a level of informality that makes the team feel included and safe. The leader listens more and talks less, giving the group more time to share insights and learnings with others. The group and the leader have started to say "we" and "us" more often.

- **PHASE 4: EMPOWERED TEAM.** The fourth phase of team building begins to harness the collective focus and efforts of the entire team. The team leader transfers decision making and authority to the team. Self-less action is commonplace, and the team begins to build similar links to external stakeholders, based on the same values of connection, achievement, respect, and empowerment. Communication is candid; empathy is the rule; the tone is friendly and open; debate is frequent but civil. New teammates' input is valued, and people freely own up to their mistakes. Accountability is high, and teammates are routinely recognized for their contributions, sometimes formally but often casually. In this stage, the leader proactively seeks to improve skills of teammates through internal and external learning and on-the-job training. New team members partner with experienced ones to accelerate learning and provide encouragement. The leader pushes decision making down to the team and engages team members in open-ended discussions about their professional and personal development.

- **PHASE 5: THE 10X ADVANTAGE (AKA THE UNSTOP-PABLE TEAM).** This is the peak of team building. The CARE loop has become a well-oiled machine within the team as members seek to activate the CARE loop with external constituents as well. The team reaches levels of performance that have not been seen before and enjoys spending time together at work or for fun, and word-of-mouth about the team's commitment to each other and to their goals spreads far and wide. The leader is humble; humor and warmth abound. The team's actions are magnified and improved by the support and participation of their contributors, customers, and community. The team's three stakeholders regularly provide feedback and new ideas to support the team's goals and join in celebrations of the team's efforts. People express enthusiasm, even love, for each other, and look for new opportunities to collaborate and pursue even bigger goals. The team develops a reputation for excellence. Potential new teammates, business partners, customers, and community members line up to get involved.

If this sounds too good to be true, I can assure you that it's not, though I do acknowledge that it's rarer than it should be. Unfortunately, most people in leadership positions settle for reaching phases one and two, not realizing how much more their teams would be capable of if only they were able to lead them through all five phases of this process. They manage "their" people to ensure that the job gets completed on time with satisfactory results. Their people work within their defined jobs, do what is asked of them, show up and leave on time, and then move to the next task. The leader (who is really acting like a manager) spends lots of time keeping everyone in line, avoiding risk, and managing up. Everything is fine, but since when is "fine" good enough?

THE 12TH-PLAYER EFFECT

Consider how the Seattle Seahawks created the 10x advantage. Obviously, because they are a professional football team, their coaches have the pick of some of the best athletes to play the game. So does everyone else in the league. What makes their story so compelling is that they've achieved 10x performance by doing something more: they invited their customers, contributors, and community to join their team too—to become the "12th player." (American football has eleven players on the field for each side.) Spend an afternoon driving around Seattle and its suburbs, and you'll see that number displayed on flagpoles and fenceposts. You'll see banners hanging from apartments, skyscrapers, and warehouses; you'll be surrounded by vehicles displaying the number 12 on license plates, tailgates, and truck hitches. You'll even see some Seahawk fans proudly showing off their 12 tattoos on sunny and rainy days alike. The 12th-player idea has been a game changer ever since the Seahawks' president Mike McCormack retired the number 12 jersey on December 15, 1984. At the time, the Seahawks were a relatively new expansion team, and McCormack decided to invite fans and the community to become a part of the team. Once Microsoft billionaire Paul Allen took ownership of the team in

1996, the 12th-player focus intensified. When building the new football stadium, Allen ordered architects to design it to maximize the sound of the fans' cheers by directing the sound down to the field and even installed a sound-monitoring system to display real-time decibel levels for fans. These were just some of the tactics the team used to embrace its external "teammates."

The results are remarkable. Since 2002, the Seahawks have had a 68.75 percent winning percentage at home. Seahawk fans have earned two world records for the loudest cheering. Their most recent one occurred in 2014, reaching 137.6 decibels, just a few short of rupturing eardrums! The 12th-player effect unsettles opponents, resulting in a league high of 130 false starts by the visiting team due to the sound level. It's also been good for business. The #12 Seahawks jersey is one of the highest selling in the NFL. Stakeholders have magnified the 12th-player effect by starting businesses that support the team's outreach efforts. Joe Tafoya created an app called Volume 12 that encourages fans and the community to connect with the team. Then there are Adam Merkl and Ryan Hilliard, co-founders of Hilliard's Beer, which in 2013 began brewing a pale ale called The 12th Can. Another group of fans created a "council" to give feedback to the team. These efforts all contribute to team cohesion.

Going even further, the Seahawks created the Spirit

of 12 Partners, a collaboration with local nonprofit organizations aimed at supporting underserved members of the Seattle community, from underprivileged kids to wounded veterans. The Seahawks' customers, contributors, and community have responded with 127 (and counting) consecutive sold-out games and one of the highest season-ticket-holder annual renewal percentages in the league: 99 percent.

The 10x advantage can be found on the battlefield, too. Journalist Doug Stanton chronicled the activities of an Army Special Forces (Green Berets) unit called Operational Detachment Alpha (ODA) 595 in Afghanistan.[2] Along with a few CIA paramilitary operatives, ODA 595 was the first American military unit to fight in Afghanistan after 9/11. Army ODAs are twelve-member teams with an unusual training focus: to build relationships. Sound familiar? In this case, these twelve men, with ODA 555, were responsible for building relationships with an association of Afghan warlords. Called the Northern Alliance, these warlords commanded roughly fifteen thousand soldiers willing and able to fight the Taliban. The ODA teams faced a few challenges, of course, the first being that not all the warlords got along. The second and more critical issue? The enemy was three times larger, with more than fifty thousand combatants, and they were better armed. As Stanton told *Forbes*: "The mission lived or died on the ability of the soldiers to create rapport and relationships and to work by, with, and through their counterparts. Not over, under, or remote from. But by-with-and-through. That's their doctrine."[3]

On October 19, 2001, ODA 595 landed via helicopter in the mountains of Afghanistan. What happened next was a remarkable feat of team building and team execution. With roughly 350 Army personnel, 100 CIA operatives, and a handful of Air Force bombers supporting these teams from afar and above, they successfully teamed up with the Northern Alliance and destroyed critical Taliban strong-holds. Imagine the scene: some 500 Americans, represent-ing multiple small teams, successfully overcoming a force one hundred times its size. Of course, they didn't do it alone. The Northern Alliance, consisting of recruits from each local warlord's community, played a crucial role, helping find and target Taliban fighters. Nevertheless, the partner-ship wouldn't have been possible without the relationship-building abilities of our ODA and CIA teams.

In almost any circumstance you can envision, the 10x advantage is worth pursuing, if not downright essential for survival. Whether you look at sharing-economy companies like Airbnb and Uber, customer-driven retailers like eBay and Amazon, or social media platforms like Facebook and Twitter, every business team today must build healthy re-lationships with those inside and outside their companies. Indeed, it's often hard to tell where the company begins and ends, so rich and interdependent are these relationships. Look closely at the best companies, and you can see the CARE loop in action. In many cases, a company's competitive advantage comes from making it easy for their constituents—employees, business partners, customers, and communities—to connect, achieve, respect, and empower each other.

No wonder hospitality organizations like Marriott get this and are implementing plans built around the concept of caring. Marriott's mission is "to be the world's favorite travel company." The challenge of treating guests as friends and family is to carry that mission into some 6,500 hotels in 110 countries with over 177,000 people managing 1.1 million hotel rooms every single day of the year. It is a daunting task—affecting tens of millions of guests a year. Though cultures vary around the globe, the one common denominator in Marriott's mission is its commitment to care. But fancy mission statements go only so far. It's in the day-to-day implementation of the CARE loop within Marriott and with its external team members that the 10x advantage is realized. Marriott's approach combines the company's vision with its actions in its TakeCare Wellbeing program. It's a way of connecting, achieving, respecting, and empowering that grew out of the original vision statement of the company's founders, J. Willard Marriott and Alice Sheets Marriott, more than ninety years ago: "Take care of your associates [coworkers] and they will take care of your customers and your customers will come back."

A lot has changed since the days of a single root-beer shop at a train stop in Maryland, but Marriott's guiding principles haven't changed. They have become more formalized through TakeCare, which addresses four recipients of care: the individual, workers at all levels, customers (owners, franchisees, and guests), and the community. TakeCare, encompassing physical, emotional, financial, and professional well-being, is first and foremost directed at the company's associates. It formalizes the SEAL Team motto, "I've got your back." This holistic program starts by helping individuals lead themselves. It also provides associates with guidance and support in managing their financial lives, developing their careers, and leading others. The caring mindset extends into the communities where Marriott operates. Associates are encouraged to participate in community-outreach programs and to express their friends-and-family orientation with outside contributors. Recently, Marriott launched a new initiative called Serve 360, which further defines how it extends care beyond the confines of the organization. Serve 360 outlines four actions: nurture, sustain, empower, and welcome, with specific long-term goals, such as committing fifteen million person-hours of volunteer time within the communities they serve. With such an authentic and consistent focus on embracing care in every facet of the business, it's no wonder Marriott has been chosen twenty years in a row (1998–2017) as a Best Place to Work, while also growing its market capitalization to over $120 billion in 2018.

THE SOFT STUFF DOESN'T HAVE TO BE HARD

Putting the four actions of the CARE loop to work might sound daunting at first, yet it will be the most rewarding experience you will ever have. *Life happens.* When it does, take a breath and know that with some care for yourself and for others, you can endure mistakes and missteps because you are surrounded by a tight-knit family, whether related by blood, emotional bonds, or both. I like to think of the people I care for, and who care for me, as my "care squad." Years after the members of my various care squads have come together and then gone their separate ways, I still know that we have one another's back and that the experiences I had with those incredible people will stay with me forever.

Which brings me to the hardest part of team building: saying good-bye. All good things come to an end, and the same holds true for teams. It's a natural process in the team-building cycle to disband, rebuild, renew, and ramp up for another challenge. Very few teams stay intact after goals are achieved; in fact, many teams rotate members on and off their rosters even at the height of their accomplishments.

Here's the lesson I've learned about disbanding: factor in time for the team to grieve. For many, the team they've just been a part of is unlike any experience they've had before. They are emotionally connected to the team and their teammates. Losing these connections is painful. Don't be surprised if some of your teammates experience temporary situational depression, as clinicians refer to it. With every ending, there is a loss, even if there are good reasons for and even excitement about moving on.

When the time comes to dissolve the team, make a party out of it. Give people different assignments to make the parting ceremony memorable and personal, from coordinating a potluck meal to collecting and sharing pictures, quotations, funny stories, and major milestones. Give everyone the chance to say their good-byes, to express their gratitude, and to celebrate the experience. Don't be alarmed if there are tears. Stretch out your arms for a lot of hugs, too. Finally, don't be shy about staying in touch or trying to help your teammates even after you've officially disbanded. In SEAL Team, I made it my mission to help every one of my platoon mates find the jobs or opportunities they were looking for. For some it was a simple process of providing a recommendation; for others it required helping to reposition them for their next roles. One of my proudest moments was helping a petty officer second class with his Seaman to Admiral application (a unique Navy opportunity whereby select enlisted sailors can become officers). KD, as we called him, earned the appointment and today is a senior-ranking Navy SEAL officer leading an entire SEAL Team. Likewise, when members of my Perfect Pushup team decided it was time to move on, I lent a hand in helping them find new teams to join.

Your care doesn't end when the goal is accomplished. As the leader, it's your responsibility to take care of your teammates when breaking the team apart. Years later, you might even be called upon to keep caring for their well-being in the form of writing a letter of recommendation or making time for a reference interview. This comes with the territory for CARE-based leading. Your care never stops. Guess what else happens? The care you bestowed upon your teammates gets passed along, as they embark on their own team-building journeys and take that same caring approach to their new endeavors. There is no greater satisfaction than knowing you made a difference by helping others make a difference too.

CONCLUSION

My first best friend growing up was my grandmother Priscilla Alden Mills, known to me as Gramz. She lived about three miles away on a farm with horses, chickens, dogs, a vegetable garden, a pond, and, most important, trucks and tractors. It was my home away from home growing up. She introduced me to a lot of "firsts" in my life, such as sautéed Cheerios with whole butter (my breakfast favorite); driving a jeep, truck, and tractor (all first performed while sitting on her lap); riding a horse; jumping in manure; and removing lots of rocks from her vegetable garden while she worked the rototiller.

She was full of energy and constantly on the go, and I loved playing the role of her helper. Frequently that put me in some awkward situations. It was more like being an accomplice to petty crimes. In the fall, I spent many weekends sitting in the back of her 1960s turquoise-and-white Ford F-100, picking up other people's trash. She loved tending her garden, and fall was prime time for collecting compost. We would race around my friends' neighborhoods picking up their bags of leaves before the garbage trucks did. I thought it was a normal weekend activity, including the part when surprised neighbors rushed out their front doors toward Gramz's truck, thinking we were stealing something. We had some crazy times together, but there was always one thing I could count on from Gramz: hugs. Gramz was a hugger.

She hugged her dogs (all ten of them, mostly strays), her horses, and of course her grandsons, my brother Andrew and me. She hugged me so often that I just assumed it was a normal greeting: say hello and then hug it out. I never thought much of her hugging habit until she was diagnosed with a form of dementia. Our family did the best we could to remind her of all the memories we had made together. We placed photographs of our nutty adventures all around her house, with our names posted on them as prompts. That helped for a while, but eventually those memories faded for her. But one thing didn't: her response to a hug. As I put my arms around her, she smiled and squeezed me right back. It was the only form of communication we had during those final months, and I never missed an opportunity to hug her. Those hugs at the end of her life were especially powerful because they reminded me that, even after her mental capabilities had faded, Gramz's instincts to love and be loved were intact. So it is with all of us.

You might think that there's no room for hugging in a platoon of SEALs, but you'd be wrong. I'm a huge hugger (thanks, Gramz). We are *all* huge huggers. Yes, that's right: America's fiercest warriors are huggers; we hugged it out all the time. And it isn't just SEALs. I've witnessed it in all branches of the military. You know why? Because we love each other. No, seriously, we do. Ever had the chance to chat with a Congressional Medal of Honor recipient? I've talked to several, and they all say the same thing about their acts of heroism: they stepped up because they loved their teammates and didn't want to let them down. There's that word again: *love*.

To be honest, during all my time in the SEALs, I was never interested in dying for my country; I was, however, willing to die for my teammates, and I knew they were willing to die for me. It's not that we don't love our country—we do—but "country" is such a large, amorphous concept; it's hard to connect with it on a personal level, as you do with your teammates. The same thing can be said of a corporation, a sports team, or a charity. It is hard for people to relate to an entire organization, which might represent thousands or millions of people. When you think back on your proudest or hardest moments, you probably think of *people*—from childhood, school, a weekend road trip, your first job, other jobs, and probably the one you're in right now—and you realize how many people have had your back during these times. You probably don't think, first and foremost, of the institutions—colleges, military academies, blue-chip companies, or community organizations—where those relationships were formed. But those huggers? They're impossible to forget, because team building and teamwork are personal. They're about a group of human beings, all with their own quirks of personality, their own superpowers and weaknesses, coming together to do something amazing. It might be raising money for a local nonprofit, coaching your kids' soccer team, leading a new product to market, convincing the bank not to call in your loan, or helping capture a war criminal. But the work of teams—and the work of leadership required to build unstoppable teams—comes down to nothing less than love and, yes, lots of hugs—to celebrate, to commiserate, to remind friends that you've got their back, and even to say good-bye when the mission is complete.

Making this happen is messy. There's no app for it. How do you learn it? Well, you can read this book, of course, and glean inspiration and insights from the experience (mine and others') I share with you here. You can put the CARE loop to work and practice connecting, achieving, respecting, and empowering. Honestly, though, you'll just have to give it a shot; try it out and see how it feels. Have some faith that you've done the work, or that you're prepared to do the work, of opening yourself and your heart to building relationships that are deep, sturdy as hell, and immensely satisfying to your heart and your head.

My most terrifying moment in SEAL training was my first jump, at fourteen thousand feet, during special-operations military free fall (MFF) training. It wasn't the height that scared me. I had jumped out of airplanes and helicopters more than fifty times before. What terrified me about this jump was that it was the first time I was jumping with a parachute I had packed *myself.* We'd had lots of prior training on how to pack our own parachutes, and yet I had a nagging belief that I just plain sucked at folding things. That belief came from the fact that I failed pretty much every room inspection at the Naval Academy. Really, I was terrible at making my bed. I could never get those hospital corners just right. Making my socks "smile" and my towels line up neatly was just beyond me.

So here I am at four thirty in the morning on the ramp of a C-130 looking out over the mountain range surrounding Yuma, Arizona. I'm watching the sun come up at fourteen thousand feet. The engines roar so loudly that we have to shout, using short, simple phrases and hand signals to be understood. My eyes are glued to the red jump light. When it turns green, it will be my turn to jump.

My instructor turns to me and shouts, "Sir, turn around and back up to the ramp!" I do as directed and stop when I think I've gone far enough.

He responds with, "Sir, put your heels over the ramp!"

I slowly edge my heels beyond the nonskid surface of the ramp. He then smiles, looks at me, and yells, "Look down!"

I'm trying to keep my balance on the balls of my feet as I cast a quick glance down past my right elbow.

He asks, "Pretty high, isn't it?"

I shoot him an oh-that's-so-not-funny smile. His next question: "Will you jump?" I slowly nod.

"Good!" he exclaims, and as the jump light turns green, he says, "Sir, you have the rest of your life to figure out how to open your parachute. Good luck!" and then pushes me off the ramp. A few seconds later, he flies down beside me, cracks a huge smile, and shouts, "Did you get it? You have about sixty seconds to pull the rip cord!"

I'm happy to report that my chute opened that day, just as it did on the subsequent fifty or so jumps I did after this one. I had learned to pack my own parachute, and each time it opened, I became more confident about my packing ability.

I end with this story for several reasons. First, team building and leading are a lot like taking that first jump. You're jumping into the unknown. It's scary, but you jump anyway. Second, we are all, in effect, packing our own parachutes. You may never find yourself on the ramp of a C-130 at fourteen thousand feet, but it may feel just like that when you're faced with the task of building a team to conquer a seemingly impossible obstacle. Each time you pack that parachute, you get better, more confident, and more skilled. Each jump gets a little easier.

There are three basic ways you can jump off the ramp: (1) be pushed, as I was the first time; (2) squat down and timidly stick one foot over the edge in an effort to get a little closer to earth, like a child jumping off a diving board for the first time; and (3) jump headfirst. The latter is best because when you jump headfirst you *have* to commit. Your body follows your head, and you dive out looking just like Superman flying over a building. When there's a whole team jumping off at once, do you know how motivating it is to watch all your teammates diving off the ramp? If you're the last one to jump, you're literally running off the ramp and diving to catch up with them. That's what it's like to be all in. That's what it's like to be part of an unstoppable team. There are all kinds of challenges to be solved in this world, and there are all kinds of talented people waiting to team up to solve them. The question is, who will take that first jump to lead them?

The jump light for building your team has just turned from red to green. Your teammates are waiting . . . waiting for you to take that first step.

You *are* ready. The time is now. Go! Go! Go!

ACKNOWLEDGMENTS

Writing a book is a lonely endeavor. It involves long periods of solitary confinement. I find writing to be a struggle between doubts and determination, where the "whiner" is active and the "whisperer" is reticent. I suspect there are authors out there who happily sit alone and crank out page after page with relative ease. I am not that author. In fact, I don't even like working alone. For me, it's always been about the team. Every significant accomplishment in my life occurred because of a team. And though writing involves countless hours of solitude, this book is the result of an unstoppable team. Procrastination and self-doubt were my constant enemies, and we battled every morning. Thankfully I have teammates who willingly joined me in beating back these clever combatants. I could write an entire chapter on how these people helped me prevail against my toughest competitor: me. I appreciate that books rarely claim more than one author or two, but if there were enough space on the cover, I would put their names before mine. The sentences that follow are my attempt to capture the depth and breadth of my teammates' efforts to turn this book into reality.

From before sunrise to well after sunset, my swim buddy in life, Jennifer Ryan Mills, served on the front lines with me. Her calm but firm guidance picked me up when I was down. She cleared the writing decks for months on end while keeping the family ship, with four high-energy boys, on course. This book would not have happened without her steadfast support and continually whispering, "Keep going." On that end, my team leaders in training—Henry, Charlie, John, and William—were remarkably supportive while Dad toiled away in the "writing box" (a closet with a small desk and bathroom). They played just outside the writing box and rarely complained of my absence. I often heard their voices—the laughter, tears, and cheers—and through it all their constant encouragement fueled me to press on.

While my family inspired me to keep trying, another teammate challenged me to try harder. My editor, Hollis Heimbouch, aka Super H, of Harper Business, and her amazing team were my swim buddies from start to finish. In particular, Super H is always upbeat while pressing me to do more than I originally thought possible. She cares. She is the definition of a care-based leader who has your back. She has this uncanny ability to take a jumbled-up, poorly written idea and rephrase it just how I meant to write it the first time. As lonely as writing is, I didn't feel alone with her (and her teammates!) at the editing helm.

Then there's my agent, Jud Laghi, aka J-Train. It's the perfect nickname for him. He's a diesel locomotive engine that never quits. He powers up the hills and keeps things moving forward. He is tireless and he delivers. Throughout this book-writing journey, he served many roles, but none was more important than being there to answer my call. Like my other teammates, he has my back, and I feel fortunate to have him as a friend, colleague, and swim buddy.

Speaking of getting things done on time, if J-Train is the locomotive, then the engineer has to be Mama Monaco, my manager, Carolyn Monaco. Well before this book was even a proposal, she was the one who kept whispering, "Take another step . . . and let me show you how." Mama made the introductions, set the course, and showed me how to execute it. This book is but one of the by-products of her tutelage and, as with the others in this section, I remain eternally grateful for her support and for her belief in me.

Every train needs a conductor to keep things running on time, and my conductor is Barbara Caraballo, aka Super Bee (SB). I often refer to her as my angel in the sky, for though I rarely see her (we live three thousand miles apart), she's always there—just a phone call, e-mail, or text away. She keeps the trains running on time, all the time. She's a bundle of positive can-do attitude that was instrumental in getting the *i*'s dotted and the *t*'s crossed for this book . . . and so much more.

My wife and boys, Super H (and the entire Harper team), J-Train, Mama, and SB are my teammates, but others shaped me and provided the lessons learned to create this book. Kent School Boat Club (KSBC), with Coaches Hart Perry and Eric Houston, where I learned the craft and power of teamwork. Navy Crew with Coaches Rick Clothier and Rodney Pratt, who taught me how to shift focus from selfishness to selflessness. SEAL Team with Commanding Officers Doug Lowe, David Morrison, and Chuck Lockett along with my chiefs, LPOs, and platoon mates—the greatest collection of teammates I've ever experienced. Team Perfect from the earliest days with my first entrepreneurial swim buddy, Mark Friedman, to swim buddies Andrew Morrison, Ian Coats MacColl, Christa Skov, Valerie O'Brien, and Dave Hollister—we prevailed against all odds time and time again. I refer to them as my "Civilian SEAL Team," for when I worked with them, there were no obstacles, only opportunities.

Of course, no acknowledgments are ever complete without a callout to my parents. I'm fortunate to have two sets: Mom and Dad and Mumzie and Pops. To my parents who tirelessly whispered, "You can do it . . . it's up to you . . ." This book would never have been written without their continual suppression of my earliest encounters with the whiner. They represent the voice of my first whisperer, which set me on a course that forever changed my life. And my other set of parents—I don't view them as in-laws—Mumzie and Pops represent another team of whisperers that amplify the original whisperers in my life and, like the others mentioned here, always remain at the ready to support, encourage, and at just the right times say something similar in theme to what my military free-fall instructor said: "Time to jump. Go! Go! Go!"

> With gratitude, love, and respect
> to all of my teammates,
> *Alden*

NOTES

CHAPTER 1: YOUR PLATFORM

1. Nancy F. Koehn, "Leadership Lessons from the Shackleton Expedition," *New York Times*, Dec. 24, 2011, https://www.nytimes.com/2011/12/25/business/leadership-lessons-from-the-shackleton-expedition.html.
2. "James E. Burke, MBA 1949: 2003 Alumni Achievement Award Recipient," Harvard Business School, Jan. 1, 2003, https://www.alumni.hbs.edu/stories/Pages/story-bulletin.aspx?num=2016.
3. Mukul Pandya et al., *Nightly Business Report Presents Lasting Leadership: What You Can Learn from the Top 25 Business People of Our Times* (Philadelphia: Wharton School Publishing, 2004), 41.
4. In his book *Brain Rules: 12 Principles for Surviving and Thriving at Work, Home, and School* (Seattle: Pear Press, 2014), on page 5, John Medina wrote, "Our brains actually were built to survive in jungles and grasslands. We have not outgrown this."

CHAPTER 3: CONNECT

1. Gallup Poll, "State of the American Workplace," 2017. Retrieved on Sept. 24, 2018, from https://news.gallup.com/reports/199961/7.aspx.

2. Mike Krzyzewski, *Leading with the Heart: Coach K's Successful Strategies for Basketball, Business, and Life* (New York: Warner Books, 2000), 153–54.

3. Naomi Eisenberger and George Kohlrieser, "Lead with Your Heart, Not Just Your Head," *Harvard Business Review*, Nov. 16, 2012, https://hbr.org/2012/11/are-you-getting-personal-as-a.

CHAPTER 5: RESPECT

1. Christine Porath, "Half of Employees Don't Feel Respected by Their Bosses," *Harvard Business Review*, Nov. 19, 2014, https://hbr.org/2014/11/half-of-employees-dont-feel-respected-by-their-bosses.

2. Porath, "Half of Employees Don't Feel Respected."

3. Terry Waghorn, "How Employee Engagement Turned Around Campbell's," *Forbes*, June 23, 2009, https://www.forbes.com/2009/06/23/employee-engagement-conant-leadership-managing-turnaround.html#4a7a2a762ec0.

4. Waghorn, "How Employee Engagement Turned Around Campbell's."

5. John Wooden with Steve Jamison, *Wooden: A Lifetime of Observations and Reflections On and Off the Court* (New York: McGraw-Hill, 1997), 199.

6. Neil Hayes, *When the Game Stands Tall: The Story of the De La Salle Spartans and Football's Longest Winning Streak* (Berkeley, CA: North Atlantic Books, 2012), 11.

7. Caryn Davies, "Tom Terhaar: Keeper of Dreams," *Row 360*, May 30, 2018, http://row-360.com/tom-terhaar-keeper-dreams.

8. Steve Politi, "Rio 2016: How a Rutgers Grad Built a Great U.S. Olympic Dynasty in Rowing," NJ.com, Aug. 14, 2016, https://www.nj.com/olympics/index.ssf/2016/08/rio_2016_how_a_rutgers_grad_built_a_great_us_olympic_dynasty_politi.html.

9. Davies, "Tom Terhaar."

10. Associated Press, "America's Unsung Dynasty: The Women's 8 of Rowing," *USA Today*, June 15, 2016, https://www.usatoday.com/story